amy butler's
style stitches

amy butler's
style stitches
12 easy ways to 26 wonderful bags!

photographs by david butler

CHRONICLE BOOKS
SAN FRANCISCO

Art Direction by Amy and David Butler
Designed by Design at NOON
Technical writing by Dianne Barcus and Kim Ventura
Styling by Nora Corbett

Coats Dual Duty XP is a registered trademark of Coats & Clark Inc. Pellon Fusible Thermolam Plus, Pellon Shape Flex, and Peltex are registered trademarks of Freudenberg Nonwovens. Prym-Dritz is a registered trademark of the Prym-Dritz Corp.

Manufacturer's instructions for Pellon Thermolam Plus Fusible, Pellon Shape-Flex SF-101, Pellon Peltex 70 Sew-In Ultra-Firm Stabilizer, Pellon Peltex 71F Single-Sided Fusible Ultra-Firm Stabilizer, and Pellon Peltex 72F Double-Sided Fusible Ultra-Firm Stabilizer on page 172 printed with permission of manufacturer.

Library of Congress Cataloging-in-Publication Data available.

ISBN 978-0-8118-6669-9

Manufactured in China.

10 9 8 7 6 5 4 3 2

Chronicle Books LLC
680 Second Street
San Francisco, California 94107
www.chroniclebooks.com

Contents

Introduction

12 easy ways to 26 wonderful purses and handbags!

If you've picked up this book, chances are you love handbags as much as I do. I built my sewing-pattern business around creating designs for bags that are stylish, diverse, and personal—and personality has everything to do with personal style. Creating your own garments, home décor, and, yes, handbags is the ultimate way to set yourself apart, tell your story, and share your creative voice with the world.

I designed these projects with ease and simplicity in mind, giving you a few well-crafted foundations with lots of options. Starting with twelve "foundation" bag designs, I developed unique and stylish elements to help you create different looks. Most of the bags have several variations and an array of great detailing to help you inject your distinctive style because in the end, it is really about *your* personality shining through.

I organized the book so it starts with the easiest project and ends with the most complex (although it is still well-suited for the intermediate seamstress). If you are new to sewing, you can work your way through the book and watch your skills grow as you move from project to project. Just because a project is easy doesn't mean the design needs to be basic. You'll find in these designs that simplicity never sacrifices great style!

I encourage you, especially if you are new to sewing, to begin by reading Getting Started (page 13). In this section, you'll find great tips on materials, tools, and fabrics, as well as measurement guidelines that will prove invaluable. Refer to Glossary & Techniques (page 171) for handy sewing definitions and illustrated how-tos.

If you've purchased my patterns in the past, or my other sewing-project books, *Amy Butler's In Stitches* or *Amy Butler's Little Stitches for Little Ones,* you'll appreciate the value of being able to create stunning and personal projects for yourself and loved ones from just one book! Sewing is a timeless art, and creating fashion for yourself is the best measure of true personal style. As trends come and go, you can make yourself up to be exactly who you are, one stylish stitch at a time!

Enjoy!

—Amy

Getting Started

FABRICS

You're going out into the world with your latest creation—what will it be? Everyone will notice two things about your bag: its shape and its fabrics. Fabrics have attitude! Exciting, sophisticated, quiet, graceful, confident, and sometimes wild. You'll want different fabrics for different moods and different uses. Different bags will show the world the many wonderful facets of your personality and unstoppable creativity.

I am a fabric designer, too. You might agree with me that the best part of designing a new bag is deciding which fabrics to use. You'll have practical things to consider as well. For example, can you use certain weight fabrics for different styles and sizes of bags? Do you want Home Dec weight versus quilting and/or fashion weight? Can you combine vintage fabric with new fabric? Some vintage fabrics may be too fragile for a heavily used shopper. Proper interfacings and good technique in hems and seams are always needed, but they can't help worn or deteriorating fabric thread. I would suggest using common sense, except that I readily eschew common sense if the fabric is just too fantastic! Besides, you can always get creative and sew a sturdy lining or an extra panel to reinforce your grandmother's prom dress turned new shoulder bag.

If you're new to sewing, choosing fabrics can be an overwhelming prospect. No worries! Here are some rules of thumb to keep in mind before you select and buy fabrics, and some tips for preparation and care before you start sewing:

• Carefully read the Materials List for your project and make sure you have an understanding of the type of weight fabric you'll need to use. Keep in mind that you can adjust interfacing amounts to achieve your desired thickness, sturdiness, and weight. If you are repurposing vintage materials, be sure to use fabric pieces that are still in good shape: no worn spots or weak areas.

• If you are working with a fabric with a directional print, be sure to purchase enough yardage to allow for matching up repeats in the fabric and to keep the designs all going in the same direction on the various parts of your project.

• As for color and pattern selection, always follow your instincts. You want to work with prints that you love, Love, LOVE! You'll be investing a good amount of time in your project, so have fun and combine surprising colors and designs.

• Be sensitive to texture, fiber, and weight differences. Make sure you are combining compatible fabrics. For example, avoid mixing lightweight, airy cottons with big, heavy wools; the dramatically different textures and weights will diminish the quality of your project, plus these fabrics have different washing needs. If you stay roughly within the same weight, fiber family, or texture, you'll be good to go. You can successfully marry a lighter-weight cotton to a heavier cotton providing you add additional interfacing to the lighter-weight fabric so it is balanced with the heavier material.

• It is important to prewash all of your materials before you start sewing to ensure you'll have correct measurements with your fabric cuts. Most cottons and linens can be machine washed in cold water on a gentle cycle. Dry in a warm but not-too-hot dryer. Some shrinkage with most fabrics is absolutely normal. The materials lists in this book accommodate this fluctuation.

• If you are working with a vintage material, take a bit more care and caution when washing it. Most cottons can be washed cold on a gentle cycle. If your fabric hasn't been exposed to water in a while, soak it in cold water for a day or so to rehydrate the fibers before you clean it. If the fabric seems too fragile to go in the washing machine, yet you just have to use it, hand wash the material in warm water with a mild, phosphate-free soap; gently rinse; and let air dry.

NOTIONS AND TRIMS

Embellishment is part of the fun and personality inherent in your design. Just the right splash of color on a button or the perfect texture fringe can transform your finished piece. Keep your eyes peeled at antique shops, garage sales, flea markets, and fabric stores for vintage ribbons, buttons, beads, and trims. Old English buttons or Indian ribbons and trims can lend old-world charm to your modern bag. To change the mood of a simple handbag, I sometimes accent with a vintage brooch or pin from my antique costume jewelry collection.

BASIC TOOLS NEEDED FOR EACH PROJECT

• Fabric marker or chalk pencil
• Iron and ironing board
• Pressing cloth
• Ruler and tape measure
• Scissors
• Straight pins
• Turning tool (such as a closed pair of scissors)

GENERAL NOTES FOR ALL PROJECTS

• Be sure to have the basic tools on hand before beginning a project. See Basic Tools Needed for Each Project (above). Additional tools needed are listed at the beginning of each project.

• See Fabric Reference Guide (page 175) for a list of the specific fabrics used in each project.

• Terms defined in Glossary & Techniques (page 171) are marked with an asterisk (*) the first time they appear in a project.

• Preshrink your fabric by washing, drying, and pressing it before starting the project.

• All seam allowances are $1/2$" (1.3 cm) unless otherwise stated. The $1/2$" (1.3 cm) seam allowance is included in the pattern pieces and all cutting measurements.

• Follow the manufacturer's instructions closely when applying fusible interfacing and fleece. If you experience any puckering of the fabric, gently pull back the interfacing or fleece while it is still warm and reapply. Use a damp pressing cloth and the "wool" setting on your iron during the application.

PROJECT:

01

TITLE:

Cosmo Bag

A large button keynotes this wonderfully roomy and super-easy-to-make bag for today's runabout. Two styles—a shoulder bag and a handbag—let you create a unique version for different uses. It's a lot of bang (and bag) for the buck!

FINISHED SIZES	**Bag with short handle**

FINISHED SIZES

Bag with short handle

21" (53.3 cm) across the widest point [14¼" (36.2 cm) wide across the bottom] x 22½" (57.2 cm) tall with handles x 4" (10.2 cm) deep

Bag with long handle

21" (53.3 cm) across the widest point [14¼" (36.2 cm) wide across the bottom] x 26" (66 cm) tall with handles x 4" (10.2 cm) deep

FABRICS

From 44" (112 cm) wide light- to mid-weight fabric

• 1⅜ yd (1.26 m) of one print for the exterior

• 1¼ yd (1.14 m) of a coordinating solid for exterior bands, long or short handle, side pocket lining, button, and button loop

• 1⅜ yd (1.26 m) of a second coordinating print for the lining

OTHER SUPPLIES

• 6¼ yd (5.72 m) of 20" (50.8 cm) wide fusible woven interfacing (I use Shape Flex SF-101 by Pellon)

• ¼ yd (0.22 m) of 44" (112 cm) wide fusible fleece (I use fusible Thermolam Plus by Pellon)

• One 1½" (3.8 cm) button to cover (I use Prym-Dritz brand)

• 1 spool coordinating all-purpose thread (I use Coats Dual Duty XP)

See Basic Tools Needed for Each Project (page 14).

ADDITIONAL TOOLS NEEDED

• Pencil
• Wax-free tracing paper (I use Prym-Dritz brand)
• Hand sewing needle

Follow these instructions to make the bag with either the long or the short handles.

1   CUT OUT THE PATTERN PIECES.

From the pattern sheet included with this book, cut out

- Main panel
- Side panel
- Band
- Handle
- Side pocket/side pocket lining panel
- Lining/inside pocket panel

2   CUT OUT ALL OF THE PIECES FROM THE FABRIC.

From the print exterior fabric

a. Lay the fabric in a single layer with the **Right** side down. Fold one selvage edge* over 13″ (33 cm) toward the **Wrong** side and fold the opposite selvage edge over 4″ (10.3 cm).

- Cut 2 main panels on the fold* from the 13″ (33 cm) folded side
- Cut 2 side panels on the fold from the 4″ (10.3 cm) folded side

b. Fold the side pocket lining panel pattern piece back at the dashed line to use for the side pocket panel pattern piece.

- Cut 2 side pocket panels on the fold

c. Open the fabric. Using a ruler and fabric marker, measure and mark the dimensions for the bottom panel directly onto the **Right** side of a single layer of fabric. Cut along the marked lines.

- Cut 1 bottom panel: 6″ (15.2 cm) wide x 15$\frac{1}{4}$″ (38.7 cm) long

From the solid exterior fabric

d. Fold the fabric in half lengthwise, **Wrong** sides together, matching the selvage edges.

- Cut 2 bands on the fold
- Cut 2 side pocket lining panels on the fold
- Cut 8 handles: for long handles, use the entire pattern piece; for short handles, fold the pattern piece back at the dashed line

e. Open the fabric. Measure and mark the dimensions directly onto the **Right** side of a single layer of fabric. Cut along the marked lines.

- Cut 1 button loop: 5″ (12.7 cm) wide x 12″ (30.5 cm) long
- Cut 1 circle [2$\frac{1}{2}$″ (6.4 cm) diameter] to cover the button

From the lining fabric

f. Fold the fabric in half lengthwise, **Wrong** sides together, matching the selvage edges, and gently press a crease. Open the fabric. Fold the selvage edges in to meet the crease with the **Wrong** sides together. This will give you enough folded edges to cut out the lining panels, side panels, and pocket panels.

- Cut 2 lining panels on the fold
- Cut 2 side panels on the fold
- Cut 4 inside pocket panels on the fold (fold the lining panel pattern piece back at the dashed line)

g. Open the fabric. Measure and mark the dimensions for the bottom panel directly onto the **Right** side of a single layer of fabric. Cut along the marked lines.

• Cut 1 bottom panel: 6″ (15.2 cm) wide x 15$\frac{1}{4}$″ (38.7 cm) long

From the fusible interfacing

h. Use the panels you have cut as full-size pattern pieces to cut out the fusible interfacing.

• Cut 2 main panels
• Cut 4 side panels
• Cut 2 side pocket lining panels
• Cut 2 side pocket panels
• Cut 2 lining panels
• Cut 2 inside pockets panels
• Cut 2 bands
• Cut 8 handles
• Cut 2 bottom panels

From the fusible fleece

• Cut 1 bottom insert: 5″ (12.7 cm) wide x 14$\frac{1}{4}$″ (36.2 cm) long

3 **APPLY THE FUSIBLE INTERFACING AND FLEECE.**

Note: See page 172 for interfacing application tips.

a. Place the **Wrong** side of the first exterior main panel onto the fusible side of the coordinating interfacing piece. Using a damp pressing cloth*, fuse the interfacing in place. Turn the panel over and press it again, making sure there are no puckers.

b. Repeat step 3a to apply the corresponding interfacing pieces to the second main panel, both exterior and lining side panels, side pockets and pocket lining panels, bands, lining panels, lining bottom panel, 2 inside pocket panels, and all 8 handles.

c. Center the fusible side of the fleece bottom panel insert on the **Wrong** side of the exterior bottom panel. There will be $\frac{1}{2}$″ (1.3 cm) of the bottom panel showing around all edges. Place the fusible side of the interfacing over the fleece and fuse it to the **Wrong** side of the bottom panel, sealing the edges and enclosing the fleece. Turn the panel over and press it again, making sure there are no puckers.

4 **MAKE THE PLEATS ON THE MAIN PANELS.**

a. Fold the first main panel in half lengthwise, **Wrong** sides together, and place a pin at the top and bottom on the folded edge to mark the center. Then, open the panel.

b. Use tracing paper, pencil, and the pattern piece as a guide, and transfer* the pleat marks onto the **Wrong** side of the fabric. Mark along the top edge of the pattern piece onto each side of the center on the main panel.

c. Starting on the left side of the main panel, fold the panel, **Right** sides together, matching the first two pleat marks, and pin them in place. Stitch following the pleat marks, $\frac{1}{2}$″ (1.3 cm) in length. Backstitch* at each end.

d. Open the panel. Press the pleat that forms on the *interfaced* side flat, centering the fabric evenly over the stitching line. Pin and then machine baste* a 1/4" (0.6 cm) seam across the top of the pinned pleat.

e. Repeat steps 4c and 4d to make the other 3 pleats on this main panel and all 4 pleats on the second main panel.

5 ATTACH THE BANDS TO THE MAIN PANELS.

a. Place the first band and main panel **Right** sides together, matching the bottom edge of the band with the top edge of the main panel. Pin the panels in place easing the band around the curve on the main panel. Stitch a 1/2" (1.3 cm) seam along the pinned edges. Backstitch at each end.

b. Clip a small V-shape in the seam allowance* every 1/2" (1.3 cm) around the curved edge of the band to allow it to lay flat. Be careful not to clip the stitching.

c. Open the panels. On the **Wrong** side, press the seam allowances toward the band.

d. Turn the panels over to the **Right** side. Topstitch* on the band, 1/8" (0.3 cm) away from the seam that attaches it to the main panel. Backstitch at each end.

e. Repeat steps 5a through 5d to attach the second band to the second main panel.

6 ATTACH THE HANDLES TO THE MAIN PANELS/BANDS.

Note: Divide the handles into 4 sets with 2 handles each (mirror images of each other).

a. Place the left handle from the first set of handles and the main panel **Right** sides together. Match the top left edge on the main panel to the bottom edge on the handle and pin along the matched edges.

b. Stitch a 1/2" (1.3 cm) seam across the pinned edge, easing the edges around the slight curve. Backstitch at each end.

c. Open the panels. On the **Wrong** side, press the seam allowances toward the handle.

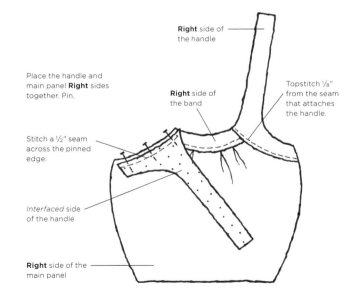

Right side of the handle

Place the handle and main panel **Right** sides together. Pin.

Right side of the band

Topstitch 1/8" from the seam that attaches the handle.

Stitch a 1/2" seam across the pinned edge.

Interfaced side of the handle

Right side of the main panel

Figure 1

d. Turn the panels over to the **Right** side again. Topstitch on the handle $\frac{1}{8}$" (0.3 cm) away from the seam that attaches it to the main panel. Backstitch at each end.

e. Repeat steps 6a through 6d to attach a second handle (one facing the opposite direction) to the top right edge of the first main panel.

f. Place the two handles **Right** sides together, matching the short top ends; make sure not to twist them. Pin them in place. Stitch a $\frac{1}{2}$" (1.3 cm) seam across the ends. Backstitch at each end.

g. Repeat steps 6a through 6f to attach a second set of handles to the second main panel.

h. Stay stitch* $\frac{3}{8}$" (1 cm) from the edge completely around the inside edges on both main panels with the bands and handles attached.

i. Clip* into the seam allowance every $\frac{1}{2}$" to $\frac{3}{4}$" (1.3 cm to 1.9 cm) around the curved edges of the handles and bands. Be careful not to clip the stitching.

j. Fold the clipped edges in toward the **Wrong** side on the inside edge of each handle and the top of the band, then press.

k. Set the main panels (with handles and bands attached) aside.

---

7   MAKE AND ATTACH THE SIDE POCKETS TO THE EXTERIOR SIDE PANELS.

a. Place the first side pocket and side pocket lining panel **Right** sides, together, matching the top edges, and pin them in place. Stitch a $\frac{1}{2}$" (1.3 cm) seam across the pinned edge. Backstitch at each end. Press the seam allowance toward the lining.

b. Flip the lining over the side pocket panel, folding it back at the top edge of the seam allowance toward the **Wrong** side. Match the bottom edges of the lining and side pocket panels, leaving $\frac{1}{2}$" (1.3 cm) of the lining showing across the top of the pocket. Press and pin the edges together. Then, machine baste a $\frac{1}{4}$" (0.6 cm) seam down both sides and across the bottom edges.

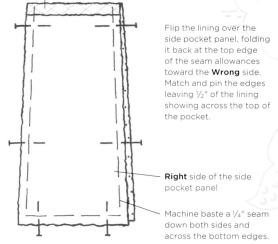

Figure 2

Right side of the side pocket lining panel

Flip the lining over the side pocket panel, folding it back at the top edge of the seam allowances toward the **Wrong** side. Match and pin the edges leaving $\frac{1}{2}$" of the lining showing across the top of the pocket.

Right side of the side pocket panel

Machine baste a $\frac{1}{4}$" seam down both sides and across the bottom edges.

c. Place the lining side of the side pocket onto the **Right** side of the first exterior side panel, matching the side and bottom edges. Pin and then machine baste a $\frac{1}{4}$" (0.6 cm) seam down the sides and across the bottom edges.

d. Repeat steps 7a through 7c to make and attach the second side pocket to the second side panel.

8   ATTACH THE EXTERIOR SIDE AND MAIN PANELS TOGETHER.

a. Place the first main and side panels **Right** sides together, matching the long side edges, and pin in place. Stitch a ½" (1.3 cm) seam down the pinned edges, beginning at the top and stopping ½" (1.3 cm) from the bottom edge. Backstitch at each end.

b. Clip into the seam allowance around the curved edge every ½" to ¾" (1.3 cm to 1.9 cm) to allow the seam to lay flat when turned **Right** side out. Be careful not to clip your stitching.

c. Repeat steps 8a and 8b to attach the second side panel to the opposite side edge of the main panel.

d. Repeat steps 8a through 8c to attach the second main panel to the opposite sides on the side panels.

e. Press all seam allowances open.

9   ATTACH THE BOTTOM PANEL.

a. Place one long edge of the exterior bottom panel and the bottom edge of one main panel **Right** sides together, matching the raw edges. Pin in place.

b. Stitch a ½" (1.3 cm) seam along the pinned edge, starting and stopping ½" (1.3 cm) from each end of the bottom panel. Backstitch at each end.

c. Turn the main panel at one of the unstitched bottom corners, matching the bottom edge of the side panel with the short edge of the bottom panel, and pin in place. Repeat step 9b to stitch them together.

d. Repeat step 9c to turn the panel at the other corners, sewing the bottom edges on the main and side panels to the other long and short side edges on the bottom panel.

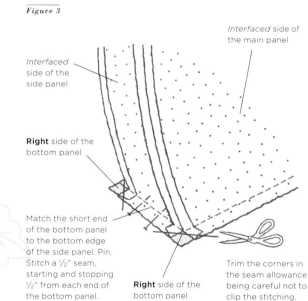

Figure 3

Interfaced side of the side panel

Interfaced side of the main panel

Right side of the bottom panel

Match the short end of the bottom panel to the bottom edge of the side panel. Pin. Stitch a ½" seam, starting and stopping ½" from each end of the bottom panel.

Right side of the bottom panel

Trim the corners in the seam allowance being careful not to clip the stitching.

e. Trim the bottom corners in the seam allowance, making sure not to clip the stitching.

f. Turn the exterior of the bag **Right** side out. Use a turning tool* to gently push out the corners, and press.

10 MAKE AND ATTACH THE INSIDE POCKETS TO THE LINING PANELS.

a. Place one inside pocket panel with interfacing attached and one without interfacing **Right** sides together. Pin along the top edges. Stitch a 1/2" (1.3 cm) seam across the pinned edge. Backstitch at each end.

b. Turn the pocket panels **Right** side out and press along the top edge.

c. Topstitch 1/2" (1.3 cm) from the top edge. Backstitch at each end.

d. Match the sides and bottom edges. Pin and then machine baste a 1/4" (0.6 cm) seam down both sides and across the bottom to hold them in place.

e. Place the pocket onto the **Right** side of the first lining panel, matching the side and bottom edges. Pin and then machine baste a 1/4" (0.6 cm) seam down both sides and across the bottom.

f. Fold the pocket and lining in half lengthwise and gently press a crease. Starting at the bottom of the pocket, stitch up along the crease to divide the pocket into two sections. Backstitch at each end.

g. Repeat steps 10a through 10f to make and attach the other inside pocket to the second lining panel.

11 MAKE THE LINING OF THE BAG.

a. Repeat steps 6a through 6j to attach the handles to each side of the lining panels.

b. Repeat steps 8a through 8e and 9a through 9e to attach the side and bottom panels to the lining panels.

12 MAKE THE BUTTON LOOP AND ATTACH IT TO THE EXTERIOR MAIN PANEL.

a. Fold the button loop piece in half lengthwise, **Wrong** sides together, and press a crease along the folded edge.

b. Open the loop. Fold each long edge in to meet the center crease, and press.

c. Fold the loop in half again at the center crease to enclose the raw edges. Press.

d. Edge stitch* down each long edge. Backstitch at each end.

e. Fold the loop in half, matching the short ends. Then, flip the end lying on top over to the side, placing the finished edges side-by-side. Overlap the side edges by 1/8" (0.3 cm) and pin them together (see figure 4 on page 29).

f. Measure and make a mark 2 3/4" (7 cm) up from the raw ends along the overlapped edges of the loop. Then, edge stitch up the overlapped edges from the raw end to the mark. Backstitch at each end.

g. Fold the top of the loop to form a triangle and press the loop flat. Edge stitch across the bottom of the triangle. Backstitch at each end.

h. Sew a gathering stitch*, 1/2" (1.3 cm) from the edge, across the raw ends of the loop. Pull the bobbin thread to gather the ends in to measure 1 1/2" (3.8 cm). Insert a straight pin at each end of the stitching line and wrap the bobbin threads around the pin in a figure 8 to hold the gathers in place.

i. Center the gathered end of the loop on the top edge on one of the bands, **Right** sides together. Pin and then machine baste the loop in place.

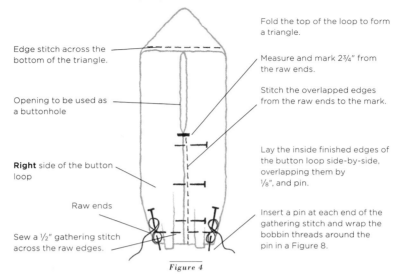

Fold the top of the loop to form a triangle.

Edge stitch across the bottom of the triangle.

Measure and mark 2¾" from the raw ends.

Stitch the overlapped edges from the raw ends to the mark.

Opening to be used as a buttonhole

Right side of the button loop

Lay the inside finished edges of the button loop side-by-side, overlapping them by ⅛", and pin.

Raw ends

Insert a pin at each end of the gathering stitch and wrap the bobbin threads around the pin in a Figure 8.

Sew a ½" gathering stitch across the raw edges.

Figure 4

13 ATTACH THE EXTERIOR AND LINING TOGETHER.

a. With the exterior **Right** side out and the lining **Wrong** side out, slide the lining over the exterior, matching the side seams. Pin them together around the outside of the handles and across the top of the side panels. Stitch a ½" (1.3 cm) seam completely around the pinned edges. Backstitch at each end.

b. Clip into the seam allowance every ½" to ¾" (1.3 cm to 1.9 cm) along each curved edge. Be careful not to clip the stitching.

c. Turn the bag **Right** side out through the opening on the inside of one of the handles, pushing the lining down inside the exterior of the bag, and press.

d. Match the exterior and lining folded edges on the inside of the first handle and pin them together. Edge stitch along the matched edges. Backstitch at each end. Repeat this step to finish the inside edges of the second handle on the back of the bag, after first pulling out the button loop.

e. Then edge stitch along the outside edges around both side panels. Backstitch at each end.

14 COVER THE BUTTON AND ATTACH IT TO THE FRONT OF THE BAG.

a. Follow the manufacturer's instructions to cover the button.

b. Measure and mark 2½" (6.4 cm) down from the top edge along the center on the front of the bag. Place the button on the mark and hand stitch it in place.

Your bag is complete! Take your Cosmo Bag to the beach, to the market, or out on the town.

02

Reversible Everyday Shopper

It's reversible (of course)! Here's a simple shopper with a few twists, including reinforced, comfy handles as well as big, sturdy pockets— one inside, one out—that swap places when the bag is reversed. Show off fabulous fabric combos in grand fashion and save on plastic bags at the store. No more blah canvas for you.

| **FINISHED SIZE** | 16" (40.6 cm) wide at bottom, 13" (33 cm) wide at top x 19" (48.3 cm) tall (not including handles) x 5½" (14 cm) deep |

FABRICS

From 54" (137 cm) wide mid-weight Home Dec fabric

• ¾ yd (0.69 m) of one print for the exterior

• 1⅝ yd (1.49 m) of a coordinating print for the reversible side, pockets, and handles

OTHER SUPPLIES

• 5½ yd (5.03 m) of 20" (50.8 cm) wide fusible woven interfacing (I use Shape Flex SF-101 by Pellon)

• ¼ yd (0.23 m) of 44" (112 cm) wide fusible fleece (I use fusible Thermolam Plus by Pellon)

• 1 spool coordinating all-purpose thread (I use Coats Dual Duty XP)

See Basic Tools Needed for Each Project (page 14).

1

CUT OUT THE PATTERN PIECES.

From the pattern sheet included with this book, cut out
• Main/pocket panel
• Side panel

2

CUT OUT ALL OF THE PIECES FROM THE FABRIC.

From the exterior fabric

a. Lay the fabric in a single layer with the **Right** side down. Fold each selvage edge*
9" (22.9 cm) in toward the **Wrong** side and gently press a crease along the folded edges.
• Cut 2 main panels on the fold*

Fold each edge of the fabric in again 4" (10.2 cm) and press a crease.
• Cut 2 side panels on the fold

b. Open the fabric. Using a ruler and fabric marker, measure and mark the dimensions for
the bottom panel directly onto the **Right** side of the single layer of fabric. Then, cut along
the marked lines.
• Cut 1 bottom panel: 6½" (16.5 cm) wide x 17" (43.2 cm) long

From the coordinating fabric

c. Lay the fabric in a single layer with the **Right** side down. Fold each selvage edge
9" (22.9 cm) in toward the **Wrong** side and gently press a crease along the folded edges.
• Cut 2 main panels on the fold
• Cut 4 pocket panels on the fold (fold the pattern piece back on the dashed line)

Fold each edge of the fabric again 4" (10.2 cm) in and press a crease.
• Cut 2 side panels on the fold

d. Open the fabric. Measure and mark the following dimensions directly onto the **Right**
side of the single layer of fabric. Then, cut along the marked lines.
• Cut 2 handles: 7" (17.9 cm) wide x 23" (58.4 cm) long
• Cut 1 bottom panel: 6½" (16.5 cm) wide x 17" (43.2 cm) long

From the fusible interfacing

e. Use the panels you have cut as full-size pattern pieces to cut out the fusible interfacing.
• Cut 4 main panels
• Cut 4 side panels
• Cut 4 pocket panels
• Cut 2 bottom panels
• Cut 2 handles

From the fusible fleece

f. Measure and mark the following dimensions directly onto the **Right** side of a single layer
of fleece. Then, cut along the marked lines.
• Cut 1 bottom panel insert: 5½" (14 cm) wide x 16" (40.6 cm) long
• Cut 2 handle inserts: 1⅝" (4.1 cm) wide x 23" (58.4 cm) long

3

APPLY THE FUSIBLE INTERFACING AND FLEECE.

Note: See page 172 for interfacing application tips.

a. Place the **Wrong** side of the first exterior main panel onto the fusible side of the corresponding interfacing. Using a damp pressing cloth*, fuse the interfacing in place. Turn the panel over and press it again, making sure there are no puckers.

b. Repeat step 3a to apply the corresponding interfacing pieces to the second main panel, both reversible main panels, all side panels, all pocket panels, both handles, and the reversible bottom panel.

c. Center the fusible side of the fleece bottom panel insert on the **Wrong** side of the exterior bottom panel. There will be ½" (1.3 cm) of the fabric showing around the outside edges. Place the fusible side of the interfacing over the fleece and fuse it to the **Wrong** side of the bottom panel, sealing the edges and enclosing the fleece. Turn the panel over and press it again, making sure there are no puckers.

4

MAKE AND ATTACH THE POCKET.

a. Place two pocket panels **Right** sides together, matching all the edges. Pin along the top edges. Stitch a ½" (1.3 cm) seam across the pinned edge. Backstitch* at each end.

b. Turn the pocket panels **Right** side out and press along the top edge.

c. Topstitch* ¼" (0.6 cm) from the top edge. Backstitch at each end.

d. Match the sides and bottom edges. Pin and then machine baste* a ¼" (0.6 cm) seam down both sides and across the bottom of the pocket panels to hold them in place.

e. Place the pocket onto the **Right** side of one of the exterior main panels, matching the sides and bottom edges. Pin and then machine baste a ¼" (0.6 cm) seam to hold the pocket in place.

5

ATTACH THE SIDE PANELS TO THE MAIN PANELS.

a. Place one main and one side panel **Right** sides together, matching the long side edges. Make sure to place the wide end of the side panel at the bottom edge of the main panel. Pin along the edge. Stitch a ½" (1.3 cm) seam down the pinned edges, beginning at the top and stopping ½" (1.3 cm) from the bottom edge. Backstitch at each end.

b. Repeat step 5a to attach the second side panel to the opposite side of the main panel.

c. Repeat steps 5a and 5b to attach the second main panel to the opposite long edges of the side panels.

d. Press all seam allowances* open.

6 ATTACH THE BOTTOM PANEL.

a. Place one long edge of the exterior bottom panel and the bottom edge of one main panel **Right** sides together, matching the raw edges. Pin along the edge.

b. Stitch a ½" (1.3 cm) seam along the pinned edge, starting and stopping ½" (1.3 cm) from each end of the bottom panel. Backstitch at each end.

c. Repeat steps 6a and 6b to attach the second main panel to the other long edge of the bottom panel.

d. Turn the bag at the bottom corners. With **Right** sides together, match the bottom edge of the first side panel to the first short end of the bottom panel. Pin it in place.

e. Stitch a ½" (1.3 cm) seam along the pinned edges, starting and stopping ½" (1.3 cm) from each end of the bottom panel. Backstitch at each end.

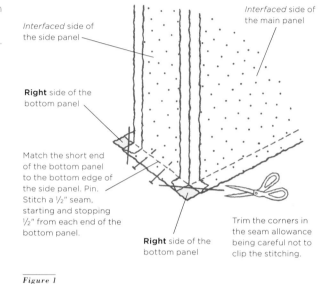

Interfaced side of the side panel

Interfaced side of the main panel

Right side of the bottom panel

Match the short end of the bottom panel to the bottom edge of the side panel. Pin. Stitch a ½" seam, starting and stopping ½" from each end of the bottom panel.

Right side of the bottom panel

Trim the corners in the seam allowance being careful not to clip the stitching.

Figure 1

f. Repeat steps 6d and 6e to attach the bottom edge of the second side panel to the other short end of the bottom panel.

g. Trim* the corners in the seam allowances, making sure not to clip the stitching.

h. Turn the exterior of the bag **Right** side out. Use your turning tool* to gently push out the corners, and press.

7 MAKE THE REVERSIBLE SIDE OF THE EVERYDAY SHOPPER.

Repeat steps 4 through 6 to make the reversible side of the bag, leaving it **Wrong** side out.

8   MAKE AND ATTACH THE HANDLES TO THE EXTERIOR.

a. Fold the first handle in half lengthwise, **Wrong** sides together, and press a crease along the folded edge.

b. Open the handle. Fold each long edge in to meet the center crease, and press. Tuck the fleece handle insert, fusible side facing down, under one of the folded edges.

c. Fold the handle in half again at the center crease to enclose the raw edges. Pin. Topstitch a ¼" (0.6 cm) seam along each folded side. Backstitch at each end. Press to fuse the fleece in place.

d. Find the center of the handle by folding it in half, matching the short raw ends. Press along the folded edge to mark the center, and open the handle. Measure and mark 1½" (3.8 cm) on each side of the center crease.

e. Fold the handle between the two marks, matching the long folded edges, and pin in place.

Figure 2

Fold the handle, matching the long folded edges, and pin in place. Stitch following original topstitching lines between the two marks.

Right side of the handle

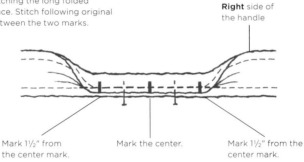

Mark 1½" from the center mark.

Mark the center.

Mark 1½" from the center mark.

f. Stitch, following the original topstitching line between the two marks. Backstitch at each end. *Note: You will be stitching through all layers of the handle, creating a 3" (7.6 cm) area that is narrower than the rest of the handle.*

g. Repeat steps 8a through 8f to make the second handle.

Mark the handle placement.

h. On the first exterior main panel, using a ruler and fabric marker, measure along the top edge, and mark 1½" (3.8 cm) in from each of the side seams. Repeat for the second exterior main panel.

i. Place one short end of the first handle on the **Right** side of the first exterior main panel with the outside edge of the handle to the inside of one of the marks. Match the ends of the handle to the top edge of the main panel. Pin and then machine baste a ¼" (0.6 cm) seam to secure the handle.

j. Place the opposite short end of the first handle to the inside of the other mark, matching the ends of the handle to the top edge of the main panel. Be careful not to twist the handle. Pin and then machine baste a ¼" (0.6 cm) seam to secure the handle.

k. Repeat steps 8i and 8j to attach the second handle to the second exterior main panel.

9 **ATTACH THE EXTERIOR AND REVERSIBLE SIDES TO COMPLETE THE BAG.**
Note: Be sure to position the exterior and reversible pockets on opposite sides of the bag.

a. With the exterior **Right** side out and the reversible side **Wrong** side out, slide the reversible piece over the exterior, tucking the handles down between the two layers.

b. Match the top edges and all seams. Pin along the top edges.

c. Stitch a ½" (1.3 cm) seam around the top of the bag, leaving the edges between the handle on one side unstitched for turning the bag **Right** side out. Backstitch at each end.

d. Turn the bag **Right** side out by pulling the exterior and reversible pieces through the opening at the top, between the handle. Push the reversible piece down inside the exterior.

e. Fold each side of the opening under ½" (1.3 cm) toward the **Wrong** side, and press. Pin the edges together.

f. Topstitch ¼" (0.6 cm) from the top edge completely around the bag to close the opening and give the Shopper a nice finished look.

Your bag is complete! Bid farewell to sad and ratty shopping bags and armloads of plastic sacks and head to the store to show off your Shopper. Different day? Turn your Shopper inside out!

03

Origami Bag Set

You can use these "anything" bags for anything and everything! Playful and practical all in one, they're a total breeze to make. I've given you six sizes from which to choose, but feel free to go wild and make them all! These pretty pouches make great gift sets or stash easily in a larger purse to get you superorganized. Whether you use them for travel, craft, sewing, knitting, or storage, you'll find yourself unfolding this pattern again and again.

FINISHED SIZES

X-small
9" (22.9 cm) wide across the top [6$\frac{1}{2}$" (16.5 cm) wide across the bottom] x 2$\frac{1}{2}$" (6.4 cm) deep x 2$\frac{3}{4}$" (7 cm) tall

Mini
10$\frac{1}{2}$" (26.7 cm) wide across the top [7$\frac{1}{4}$" (18.5 cm) wide across the bottom] x 3" (7.6 cm) deep x 3$\frac{1}{4}$" (8.3 cm) tall

Small
12$\frac{1}{2}$" (31.8 cm) wide across the top [8$\frac{1}{2}$" (21.6 cm) wide across the bottom] x 3$\frac{1}{2}$" (8.9 cm) deep x 4" (10.2 cm) tall

Medium
14" (35.6 cm) wide across the top [9$\frac{5}{8}$" (24.3 cm) wide across the bottom] x 4" (10.2 cm) deep x 5" (12.7 cm) tall

Large
16$\frac{1}{2}$" (41.9 cm) wide across the top [12" (30.5 cm) wide across the bottom] x 4$\frac{1}{2}$" (11.6 cm) deep x 6$\frac{1}{2}$" (16.5 cm) tall

X-large
17$\frac{1}{2}$" (44.5 cm) wide across the top [12$\frac{1}{2}$" (31.8 cm) wide across the bottom] x 5" (2.7 cm) deep x 7$\frac{1}{2}$" (18.5 cm) tall

FABRICS	**From 54″ (137 cm) wide mid-weight Home Dec fabric**

From 54″ (137 cm) wide mid-weight Home Dec fabric

Note: Yardage listed will make the complete set of 6 bags.

- $3/8$ yd (0.34 m) of one print for exterior panels for sizes x-small, small, and large

- $3/8$ yd (0.34 m) of a coordinating print for exterior panels for sizes x-small, small, and large

- $3/8$ yd (0.34 m) of a second print for exterior panels for sizes mini, medium, and x-large

- $3/8$ yd (0.34 m) of a second coordinating print for exterior panels for sizes mini, medium, and x-large

- $7/8$ yd (0.8 m) of a third coordinating print for the linings

---

OTHER SUPPLIES

- $2 3/8$ yd (2.17 m) of 20″ (50.8 cm) wide fusible woven interfacing (I use Shape Flex SF-101 by Pellon)

- 2 [12″ (30.5 cm)] coordinating zippers: 1 each for the x-small and mini bags (I use Coats brand)

- 2 [16″ (40.6 cm)] coordinating zippers: 1 each for the small and medium bags

- 2 [18″ (45.7 cm)] coordinating zippers: 1 each for the large and x-large bags

- 1 spool coordinating all-purpose thread (I use Coats Dual Duty XP)

See Basic Tools Needed for Each Project (page 14).

ADDITIONAL TOOLS NEEDED

- Masking tape
- Marker
- Zipper foot for your sewing machine

Follow these instructions to make any size bag. Any measurement changes will be stated in the specific step.

1

CUT OUT ALL OF THE PIECES FROM THE FABRIC.

Tip: Using a piece of masking tape and a marker, write the name of each panel and size of bag on the tape, then place it on the individual fabric pieces to identify them.

a. Using a ruler and fabric marker, measure and mark these dimensions directly onto the **Right** side of a single layer of fabric. Then, cut along the marked lines.

From the first exterior print fabric

For the x-small bag: Cut 2 panel A's: 7" (17.9 cm) wide x 5" (12.7 cm) long

For the small bag: Cut 2 panel A's: 9" (22.9 cm) wide x 6$\frac{1}{2}$" (16.5 cm) long

For the large bag: Cut 2 panel A's: 11" (27.9 cm) wide x 9$\frac{1}{2}$" (24.1 cm) long

From the first coordinating exterior print fabric

For the x-small bag: Cut 2 panel B's: 4" (10.2 cm) wide x 5" (12.7 cm) long and cut 1 tab: 2$\frac{1}{2}$" (6.4 cm) wide x 2" (5.1 cm) long

For the small bag: Cut 2 panel B's: 5$\frac{1}{2}$" (14 cm) wide x 6$\frac{1}{2}$" (16.5 cm) long and cut 1 tab: 2 $\frac{1}{2}$" (6.4 cm) wide x 2 $\frac{1}{2}$" (6.4 cm) long

For the large bag: Cut 2 panel B's: 7" (17.9 cm) wide x 9$\frac{1}{2}$" (24.1 cm) long and cut 1 tab: 2$\frac{1}{2}$" (6.4 cm) wide x 3" (7.6 cm) long

From the second exterior print fabric

For the mini bag: Cut 2 panel A's: 8" (20.3 cm) wide x 5$\frac{3}{4}$" (14.6 cm) long

For the medium bag: Cut 2 panel A's: 10" (25.4 cm) wide x 8" (20.3 cm) long

For the x-large bag: Cut 2 panel A's: 12" (30.5 cm) wide x 10$\frac{3}{4}$" (27.3 cm) long

From the second coordinating exterior print fabric

For the mini bag: Cut 2 panel B's: 4$\frac{1}{2}$" (11.4 cm) wide x 5$\frac{3}{4}$" (14.6 cm) long and cut 1 tab: 2$\frac{1}{2}$" (6.4 cm) wide x 2$\frac{1}{2}$" (6.4 cm) long

For the medium bag: Cut 2 panel B's: 6" (15.2 cm) wide x 8" (20.3 cm) long and cut 1 tab: 2$\frac{1}{2}$" (6.4 cm) wide x 3" (7.6 cm) long

For the x-large bag: Cut 2 panel B's: 7$\frac{1}{2}$" (19.1 cm) wide x 10$\frac{3}{4}$" (27.3 cm) long and cut 1 tab: 2$\frac{1}{2}$" (6.4 cm) wide x 3" (7.6 cm) long

From the lining fabric

For the x-small bag: Cut 2 panels: 10" (25.4 cm) wide x 5" (12.7cm) long

For the mini bag: Cut 2 panels: 11½" (29.2 cm) wide x 5¾" (14.6 cm) long

For the small bag: Cut 2 panels: 13½" (34.3 cm) wide x 6½" (16.5 cm) long

For the medium bag: Cut 2 panels: 15" (38.1 cm) wide x 8" (20.3 cm) long

For the large bag: Cut 2 panels: 17½" (44.5 cm) wide x 9½" (24.1 cm) long

For the x-large bag: Cut 2 panels: 18½" (47 cm) wide x 10¾" (27.3 cm) long

From the fusible interfacing

For the x-small bag: Cut 2 panel A's: 7" (17.9 cm) wide x 5" (12.7 cm) long and cut 2 panel B's: 4" (10.2 cm) wide x 5" (12.7 cm) long

For the mini bag: Cut 2 panel A's: 8" (20.3 cm) wide x 5¾" (14.6 cm) long and cut 2 panel B's: 4½" (11.4 cm) wide x 5¾" (14.6 cm) long

For the small bag: Cut 2 panel A's: 9" (22.9 cm) wide x 6½" (16.5 cm) long and cut 2 panel B's: 5½" (14 cm) wide x 6½" (16.5 cm) long

For the medium bag: Cut 2 panel A's: 10" (25.4 cm) wide x 8" (20.3 cm) long and cut 2 panel B's: 6" (15.2 cm) wide x 8" (20.3 cm) long

For the large bag: Cut 2 panel A's: 11" (27.9 cm) wide x 9½" (24.1 cm) long and cut 2 panel B's: 7" (17.9 cm) wide x 9½" (24.1 cm) long

For the x-large bag: Cut 2 panel A's: 12" (30.5 cm) wide x 10¾" (27.3 cm) long and cut 2 panel B's: 7½" (19.1 cm) wide x 10¾" (27.3 cm) long

---

2 APPLY FUSIBLE INTERFACING TO THE EXTERIOR PANELS.

Note: See page 172 for interfacing application tips.

a. Place the **Wrong** side of each exterior panel A and B onto the fusible side of the corresponding interfacing piece. Using a damp pressing cloth*, fuse the interfacing in place. Turn the panels over and press them again, making sure there are no puckers.

---

3 ATTACH PANELS A AND B TOGETHER.

Note: If you are using a directional print, organize your panels in the following manner to ensure that the seams on both sides of the bag line up. Place panel A + panel B next to each other for one side, and panel B + panel A for the other.

a. Place one panel A and one panel B **Right** sides together, matching the following raw edges for the size bag you are making.

- X-small: 5" (12.7 cm) edges
- Mini: 5¾" (14.6 cm) edges
- Small: 6½" (16.5 cm) edges

- Medium: 8" (20.3 cm) edges
- Large: 9½" (24.1 cm) edges
- X-large: 10¾" (27.3 cm) edges

Pin along the matched edges.

b. Stitch a ½" (1.3 cm) seam along the pinned edge. Backstitch* at each end. Press the seam allowance* open.

c. On the **Right** side of the panels, topstitch* ¼" (0.6 cm) on each side of the seam.

d. Repeat steps 3a through 3c to attach the second panel A and B together. Each attached panel A/B will now be referred to as an exterior panel.

4 INSTALL THE ZIPPER.

a. Place the zipper face down onto the **Right** side of the first exterior panel with the zipper head ½" (1.3 cm) from the side raw edge of panel A. Place the long edge of the zipper tape ¼" (0.6 cm) from the top edge of the panel and pin it in place.

b. Using the zipper foot for your machine, stitch ⅛" (0.3 cm) from the zipper coils, starting and stopping ½" (1.3 cm) in from each side edge of the exterior panel. Backstitch at each end.

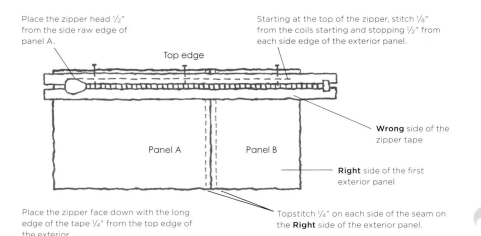

Place the zipper head ½" from the side raw edge of panel A.

Starting at the top of the zipper, stitch ⅛" from the coils starting and stopping ½" from each side edge of the exterior panel.

Top edge

Wrong side of the zipper tape

Panel A

Panel B

Right side of the first exterior panel

Place the zipper face down with the long edge of the tape ¼" from the top edge of the exterior.

Topstitch ¼" on each side of the seam on the **Right** side of the exterior panel.

Figure 1

c. Place the first lining panel **Right** sides together with the first exterior panel, sandwiching the zipper in between. Pin them in place along the top edges of the matched panels.

d. With the *interfaced* side of the exterior panel facing up, sew over the stitching that attached the zipper, starting and stopping ½" (1.3 cm) from each side edge. Backstitch at each end.

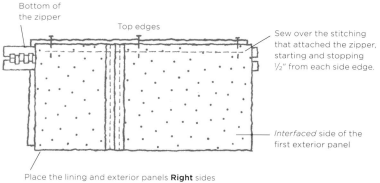

Bottom of the zipper

Top edges

Sew over the stitching that attached the zipper, starting and stopping ½" from each side edge.

Interfaced side of the first exterior panel

Place the lining and exterior panels **Right** sides together, sandwiching the zipper in between.

Figure 2

e. Flip the lining over the zipper, matching the **Wrong** sides of the lining and the exterior panels. Pin them together. Press the panels away from the zipper, pressing under the ½" (1.3 cm) unstitched fabric at each end.

f. On the **Right** side of the exterior panel, starting and stopping ½" (1.3 cm) from each side edge, topstitch ¼" (0.6 cm) from the seam that attached the zipper. Backstitch at each end.

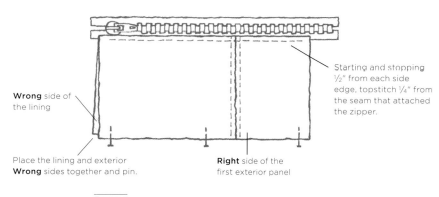

Right side of the zipper with the panels pressed away from the coils, pressing under the ½" unstitched fabric at each end.

Starting and stopping ½" from each side edge, topstitch ¼" from the seam that attached the zipper.

Wrong side of the lining

Place the lining and exterior **Wrong** sides together and pin.

Right side of the first exterior panel

Figure 3

g. Repeat steps 4a through 4f to attach the second exterior and lining panels to the other side of the zipper. Be careful not to twist the zipper. *Note: On the exterior panels, make sure to line up the seams that attach panels A and B. Position the panels across from each other.*

h. With the exterior panels facing up, lay the panels on a flat surface, spreading each set of exterior and lining panels away from the zipper. Measure $1/2$" (1.3 cm) in from the side edges along the bottom of the zipper and make a mark on the zipper coils. Bar tack* over the coils to make a new zipper stop.

i. Trim the excess zipper, leaving a 1" (2.5 cm) tail beyond the new zipper stop. Open the zipper.

5   **MAKE AND ATTACH THE TAB TO ONE EXTERIOR MAIN PANEL.**

a. Fold the tab in half lengthwise, with **Wrong** sides together, and press a crease along the folded edge.

b. Open the tab and fold each long edge in to meet the center crease, and press.

c. Fold the tab in half again at the center crease to enclose the raw edges, and press. Pin the folded edges.

d. Edge stitch* down each of the folded edges and backstitch at each end.

e. Fold the tab in half, matching the short ends, and pin.

f. On the **Right** side of one of the exterior panels, measure and mark 1" (2.5 cm) down along the side edge where the top of the zipper is located.

g. Place the pinned ends of the tab even with the side edge of the exterior panel below the mark and pin in place. Machine baste* a $1/4$" (0.6 cm) seam to secure the tab.

6   **ATTACH THE EXTERIOR AND LINING PANELS.**

Note: Leave the zipper halfway open for this step so you can turn the bag Right side out.

a. Separate the exterior from the lining panels. To keep the lining out of your way while you stitch the exterior panels, place the lining panels **Right** sides together, matching the raw edges, and pin them in place. Then fold the unstitched edges at the top of the lining panels in toward the center of the panel, and pin.

b. Place the exterior panels **Right** sides together, matching both the raw and the unstitched edges. Pin them in place. Starting and stopping at the top folded edge on each end of the zipper, stitch a $1/2$" (1.3 cm) seam down both sides and across the bottom edges. Backstitch at each end.

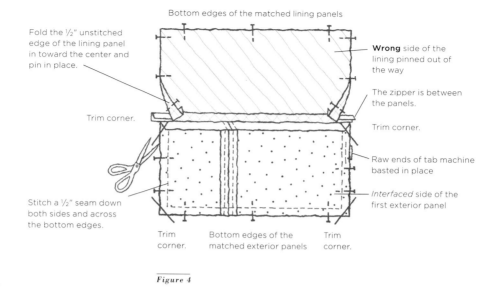

Bottom edges of the matched lining panels

Fold the ½" unstitched edge of the lining panel in toward the center and pin in place.

Wrong side of the lining pinned out of the way

The zipper is between the panels.

Trim corner.

Trim corner.

Raw ends of tab machine basted in place

Stitch a ½" seam down both sides and across the bottom edges.

Interfaced side of the first exterior panel

Trim corner.

Bottom edges of the matched exterior panels

Trim corner.

Figure 4

c. Trim* all four corners in the seam allowance, being careful not to clip your stitching. Press the seam allowances open.

d. Unpin the lining panels at each end of the zipper. Match the edges, **Right** sides together, and pin them in place. Starting and stopping just under the zipper coils, stitch a ½" (1.3 cm) seam down both sides and across the bottom edges. Leave a 4" (10.2 cm) opening centered on the bottom edge for turning the bag **Right** side out. Backstitch at each end.

e. Repeat step 6c to trim the corners, and press.

7 MAKE THE GUSSETS*.

a. With the **Right** sides of the exterior panels together, match the side and bottom seams to form a triangle in the corner. Pin the seams in place.

b. Measure and mark from the point of the corner along the side seam using the following measurements for each bag size.
- X-small: 1¼" (3.2 cm)
- Mini: 1½" (3.8 cm)
- Small: 1¾" (4.4 cm)
- Medium: 2" (5.1 cm)
- Large: 2¼" (5.7 cm)
- X-large: 2½" (6.4 cm)

c. Draw a straight line across the corner at the mark. Stitch along the marked line and backstitch at each end.

d. Trim the corner to create a ½" (1.3 cm) seam allowance.

e. Repeat steps 7a through 7d to make the gusset on the other corner of the exterior.

f. Repeat steps 7a through 7e to make the gussets on both corners of the lining.

8 COMPLETE THE BAG.

a. Turn the bag **Right** side out through the opening in the bottom of the lining.

b. Fold each edge of the opening under ½" (1.3 cm) toward the **Wrong** side, and press. Pin the edges together and edge stitch the opening closed. Push the lining down inside the exterior. Using a turning tool*, gently push out the corners.

c. Smooth the lining and exterior at the top open end of the zipper and pin them together. Topstitch across the side seam, matching the topstitching already in place. This will help hold the lining in place.

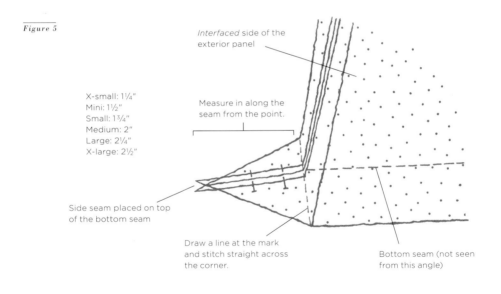

Figure 5

Interfaced side of the exterior panel

X-small: 1¼"
Mini: 1½"
Small: 1¾"
Medium: 2"
Large: 2¼"
X-large: 2½"

Measure in along the seam from the point.

Side seam placed on top of the bottom seam

Draw a line at the mark and stitch straight across the corner.

Bottom seam (not seen from this angle)

Your bags (or bag) are complete! Your quick-fix travel companions are ready to tote it all in style. Or, make them part of your home décor and store craft supplies and other this-and-thats in plain sight!

04 Beautiful Balance Checkbook Cover

After searching for the perfect checkbook cover, I simply found it best to design one. With easy-to-access panels, pockets, and keepers, this checkbook cover is a keeper. A snap closure and fine finish detailing round out the look, giving you great designer style without the designer-style price tag.

FINISHED SIZE	7" (17.9 cm) wide x 4" (10.2 cm) tall x ½" (1.3 cm) deep

= =

FABRICS

From 54" (137 cm) wide mid-weight Home Dec fabric

• ¼ yd (0.23 m) of one print for the exterior

• ¼ yd (0.23 m) of a coordinating solid for the flap

• ¼ yd (0.23 m) of a second coordinating print for the lining

- -

OTHER SUPPLIES

• ⅝ yd (0.57 m) of 20" (50.8 cm) wide fusible woven interfacing (I use Shape Flex SF-101 by Pellon)

• ¼ yd (0.23 m) of 44" (112 cm) wide fusible fleece (I use fusible Thermolam Plus by Pellon)

• ⅛ yd (0.11 m) of 20" (50.8 cm) wide Peltex #70 by Pellon or a similar extra-heavy stabilizer

• One ¾" (1.9 cm) magnetic snap (I use Prym-Dritz brand)

• 1 spool coordinating all-purpose thread (I use Coats Dual Duty XP)

See Basic Tools Needed for Each Project (page 14).

- -

ADDITIONAL TOOLS NEEDED

• Masking tape
• Marker
• Hand sewing needle

1 CUT OUT THE FLAP PATTERN PIECE FROM THE PATTERN SHEET INCLUDED WITH THIS BOOK.

2 CUT OUT ALL OF THE PIECES FROM THE FABRIC.

Tip: Using a piece of masking tape and a marker, write the name of each panel on the tape and place it on the individual fabric pieces to identify them.

a. Fold the exterior and lining fabrics in half lengthwise, **Wrong** sides together, matching the selvage edges*.

From the exterior fabric

b. Using a ruler and fabric marker, measure and mark these dimensions directly onto the fabric. Then, cut along the marked lines.
• Cut 2 main panels: 8" (20.3 cm) wide x 5¼" (13.3 cm) long

From the coordinating solid fabric

c. Lay the fabric in a single layer with the **Right** side down. Fold each selvage edge in 5" (12.7 cm) toward the **Wrong** side. This will give you enough folded edges to cut out the flaps.
• Cut 2 flaps on the fold*

From the lining fabric

• Cut 2 lining panels: 8" (20.3 cm) wide x 5¼" (13.3 cm) long
• Cut 2 inside pocket panels: 8" (20.3 cm) wide x 7" (17.9 cm) long
• Cut 1 pen holder piece: 2¾" (7 cm) wide x 5" (12.7 cm) long

d. Use the panels you have cut as full-size pattern pieces to cut out the interfacing pieces and fleece flaps.

From the fusible interfacing

• Cut 2 main panels
• Cut 2 flaps
• Cut 2 inside pocket panels

From the fusible fleece

• Cut 1 flap
• Cut 2 inside pocket inserts: 7" (17.9 cm) wide x 3" (7.6 cm) long

From the Peltex

• Cut 2 front/back pieces: 7" (17.9 cm) wide x 4" (10.2 cm) long

3

APPLY THE FUSIBLE INTERFACING.

Note: See page 172 for interfacing application tips.

a. On a flat surface, center one of the Peltex front/back pieces onto the **Wrong** side of the first exterior main panel ½" (1.3 cm) down from the top and ½" (1.3 cm) in from each side edge. This will leave ¾" (1.9 cm) exposed across the bottom edge.

b. Place the fusible side of the interfacing main panel onto the Peltex. Use a damp pressing cloth* and fuse it in place, sealing the edges around the Peltex (following the manufacturer's instructions). Turn the panel over and press it again, making sure there are no puckers.

c. Repeat steps 3a and 3b to attach the other Peltex and interfacing main panel to the second exterior main panel.

d. On the fusible side of the fleece flap, measure and mark ½" (1.3 cm) in around all of the edges. Draw a line connecting the marks. Cut along the marked lines. This will reduce bulk in the seams.

e. Place the fusible side of the corresponding interfacing onto the **Wrong** side of one flap and fuse it in place.

f. Center the fusible side of the fleece onto the *interfaced* side of the flap (there will be ½" (1.3 cm) of the fabric showing around the outside edges) and fuse it in place. Turn the flap over and press it again, making sure there are no puckers. This piece will now be referred to as exterior flap.

g. Place the fusible side of the second interfacing onto the **Wrong** side of the other flap. Fuse it in place. Turn the flap over and press it again, making sure there are no puckers. This piece will now be referred to as flap lining.

h. Place the fusible side of the corresponding *interfacing* onto the **Wrong** side of the first inside pocket panel. Fuse it in place.

i. Center one of the fleece inside pocket inserts onto the *interfaced* side of the panel, ½" (1.3 cm) from the top and side edges. This will leave 3½" (8.9 cm) exposed across the bottom edge. Fuse the fleece insert in place. Turn the panel over and press it again, making sure there are no puckers.

j. Repeat steps 3h and 3i to attach the other interfacing and fleece pieces to the second inside pocket panel.

Please set the inside pocket panels aside.

4

MAKE THE EXTERIOR.

a. Place the top edge of the exterior flap and back main panel **Right** sides together and pin them in place. Stitch a ½" (1.3 cm) seam across the pinned edge. Backstitch* at each end. Press the seam allowance* toward the main panel.

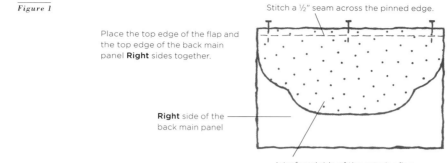

Figure 1

Place the top edge of the flap and the top edge of the back main panel **Right** sides together.

Stitch a ½" seam across the pinned edge.

Right side of the back main panel

Interfaced side of the exterior flap

b. Place the bottom edges of both main panels (the edge with ³⁄₄" (1.9 cm) exposed past the Peltex) **Right** sides together and pin them in place. Stitch a ½" (1.3 cm) seam across the pinned edge. Backstitch at each end. Press the seam allowance open.

c. Using your ruler and fabric marker, mark the placement for the magnetic snap on the **Right** side of the main panel without the flap attached. Fold the main panel in half lengthwise, matching the short side edges, and gently press a crease. Open the panel, then measure 2" (5.1 cm) down from the top edge on the center crease and make a mark.

d. Center the female half of the magnetic snap over the center crease and below the 2" (5.1 cm) mark. Install the snap following the manufacturer's instructions.

---

5   MAKE AND ATTACH THE INSIDE POCKETS TO THE LINING.

a. Fold the first inside pocket panel in half with the *interfaced* sides together, matching the 8" (20.3 cm) edges. Pin down both short side edges. Press the fold flat.

b. Topstitch* ⅛" (0.3 cm) from the folded edge. Backstitch at each end. Topstitch another row ¼" (0.6 cm) from the first and backstitch at each end.

c. Machine baste* a ¼" (0.6 cm) seam down both pinned sides and across the long edge.

d. Place the inside pocket panel on top of the **Right** side of the first lining panel, matching the top long and side raw edges. Pin and then machine baste a ¼" (0.6 cm) seam down both sides and across the long edge. (See Figure 2 on page 62.)

e. Repeat steps 5a through 5d to make and attach the second inside pocket to the bottom long edge of the second lining panel.

---

6   MAKE AND ATTACH THE PEN HOLDER TO THE LINING.

a. Fold the pen holder in half, **Right** sides together, matching the 2³⁄₄" (7 cm) edges. Pin in place. Stitch a ½" (1.3 cm) seam across the pinned edges. Backstitch at each end.

b. Turn the pen holder **Right** side out, center the seam on the pen holder panel, and press the piece flat, with the inside seam allowance open.

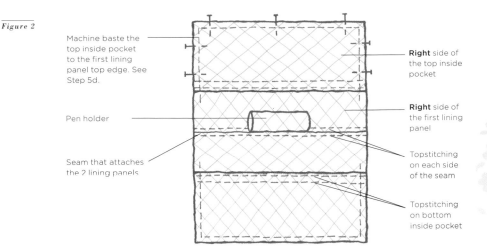

Figure 2

Machine baste the top inside pocket to the first lining panel top edge. See Step 5d.

Pen holder

Seam that attaches the 2 lining panels

Right side of the top inside pocket

Right side of the first lining panel

Topstitching on each side of the seam

Topstitching on bottom inside pocket

c. Fold the piece in half, matching the short raw ends, and pin them in place. Then, machine baste a ¼" (0.6 cm) seam across the pinned edges.

d. Place the matched edges of the pen holder onto the first lining panel and center it on the bottom long raw edge. Pin in place.

e. Place the lining panels **Right** sides together, matching the bottom edges, and pin in place. Stitch a ½" (1.3 cm) seam across the pinned edges. Backstitch at each end. Press the seam allowance open.

7 ATTACH THE FLAP LINING TO THE LINING PANELS.

a. Fold the flap lining in half, matching the side edges. Using your ruler and fabric marker, mark along the folded edge on the **Right** side to mark the center.

b. Measure and mark 1½" (3.8 cm) down from the top rounded edge along the marked center.

c. Center the male half of the magnetic snap over the center crease and below the 1½" (3.8 cm) mark. Install the snap following the manufacturer's instructions.

d. Place the long edge on the flap lining and top edge of the first lining panel **Right** sides together and pin them in place. Stitch a ½" (1.3 cm) seam, 1" (2.5 cm) in length in from each side edge. Backstitch at each end. The opening that is left will be used to turn the cover **Right** side out in step 8d.

8 ATTACH THE LINING TO THE EXTERIOR.

a. Place the lining and exterior panels **Right** sides together, matching the seams that attach the flap and the lining panels. Pin in place around the outside edges.

b. Stitch a ½" (1.3 cm) seam around the outside pinned edges of the panels and flap. Backstitch at each end.

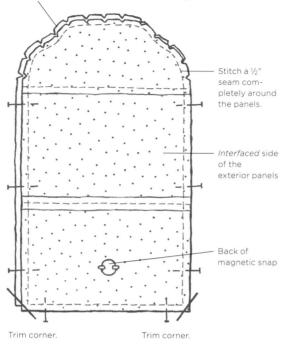

Trim the seam allowance to ¼". Then clip into it, being careful not to clip the stitching.

Stitch a ½" seam completely around the panels.

Interfaced side of the exterior panels

Back of magnetic snap

Trim corner.   Trim corner.

Figure 3

c. Trim* the corners in the seam allowances, making sure not to clip the stitching. Trim the seam allowances around the curve on the flap to ¼" (0.6 cm). Clip* into the seam allowance around the curved edges every ½" to ¾" (1.3 cm to 1.9 cm). Be careful not to clip the stitching.

d. Turn the checkbook cover **Right** side out through the opening in the seam that attaches the lining panel to the flap lining. Using a turning tool*, gently push out the corners and press the cover flat.

e. Fold each side of the opening under ½" (1.3 cm) toward the **Wrong** side and pin in place. Slipstitch* the opening closed.

f. On the exterior side, line up the seams on the front and back of the cover and pin them together. Stitch-in-the-ditch* between the seam that attaches the back panel and flap. Backstitch at each end.

g. Topstitch ¼" (0.6 cm) from the seam on the flap. Backstitch at each end. Topstitch another row ¼" (0.6 cm) from the first and backstitch at each end.

h. Topstitch ⅛" (0.3 cm) from the finished outside edges on the flap, rounding each corner. Backstitch at each end. Topstitch another row ¼" (0.6 cm) from the first and backstitch at each end.

i. Match the seams that attach the main panels together on the exterior and lining and pin them in place. On the exterior side of the cover, topstitch ⅛" (0.3 cm) on each side of the seam. Backstitch at each end. Be careful not to catch the pen holder in your stitching.

Your Checkbook Cover is complete. Now retail checkouts will get a splash of your fashion every time you go for your pen!

05

Perfectly
Pleated Clutch

Graceful and dramatic! Your friends may gasp when they learn you stitched up this amazing, sophisticated clutch. Don't sew and tell: you're the only one who needs to know it was surprisingly simple to make. Choose fabrics you adore and make different ones in the three available sizes—the smallest is designed to fit a checkbook. Everyone you know will be secretly—or not so secretly—hoping to receive one as her next gift

FINISHED SIZES	**Small clutch** 7" (17.9 cm) wide across the top [11¾" (29.8 cm) at the widest point] x 7" (17.9 cm) tall **Medium clutch** 9" (22.9 cm) wide across the top [14½" (36.8 cm) at the widest point] x 8" (20.3 cm) tall **Large clutch** 11½" (29.2 cm) wide across the top [17¼" (43.8 cm) at the widest point] x 9½" (24.1 cm) tall

═══════════════════════════════════════

FABRICS	**From 44" (112 cm) wide light- to mid-weight fabric** **For small clutch:** 1⅝ yd (1.49 m) of one print for pleated exterior **For medium clutch:** 1⅞ yd (1.71 m) of one print for pleated exterior **For large clutch:** 2⅛ yd (1.94 m) of one print for pleated exterior **Plus for any size clutch:** • ¼ yd (0.23 m) of a coordinating print for the exterior bands and handle • ⅝ yd (0.57 m) of a second coordinating print for the lining and pocket

──

OTHER SUPPLIES	**For small clutch:** • 1 yd (0.91 m) of 20" (50.8 cm) wide fusible woven interfacing (I use Shape Flex SF-101 by Pellon) • One 7" (17.9 cm) coordinating zipper (I use Coats brand) • 1 spool coordinating all-purpose thread (I use Coats Dual Duty XP) **For medium clutch:** • 1⅛ yd (1.03 m) of 20" (50.8 cm) wide fusible woven interfacing • One 10" (25.4 cm) coordinating zipper • 1 spool coordinating all-purpose thread

For large clutch

• 1¼ yd (1.14 m) of 20" (50.8 cm) wide fusible woven interfacing

• One 12" (30.5 cm) coordinating zipper

• 1 spool coordinating all-purpose thread

See Basic Tools Needed for Each Project (page 14).

ADDITIONAL TOOL NEEDED

• Zipper foot for your sewing machine

Follow these instructions to make any size clutch. Any measurement changes will be noted in the specific steps.

1

CUT OUT THE PATTERN PIECES.

From the pattern sheet included with this book, cut out

• Main/pocket panel
• Band
• Handle

2

CUT OUT ALL OF THE PIECES FROM THE FABRIC.

a. Place a single layer of the exterior fabric for the main panels **Right** side up, smoothing out any wrinkles. Using a ruler and fabric marker, measure and mark the dimensions below directly onto the fabric. Then, cut along the marked lines.

For making the pleated panel

For small clutch: Cut 2 pieces each 8″ (20.3 cm) wide x 54″ (137 cm) long
For medium clutch: Cut 2 pieces each 9″ (22.9 cm) wide x 64″ (162.6 cm) long
For large clutch: Cut 2 pieces each 11″ (27.9 cm) wide x 76″ (193 cm) long

b. Fold both coordinating band/handle and lining fabrics in half lengthwise, the **Wrong** sides together, matching the selvage edges*. Gently press a crease on the fold. Open the fabric and fold each selvage edge in toward the center crease. This will give you enough folded edges to cut out the exterior bands, handles, and lining.

From the coordinating print fabric

• Cut 2 bands on the fold*
• Cut 2 handles on the fold

From the lining fabric

• Cut 2 main panels on the fold
• Cut 2 bands on the fold
• Cut 2 pockets panels on the fold

From the fusible interfacing

c. Use the panels you have cut as full-size pattern pieces to cut out the interfacing.

• Cut 2 main panels
• Cut 4 bands
• Cut 1 pocket panel
• Cut 1 handle

3

APPLY THE FUSIBLE INTERFACING.

Note: See page 172 for interfacing application tips.

a. Place the **Wrong** side of one handle onto the fusible side of the interfacing. Using a damp pressing cloth*, fuse the interfacing in place. Turn the piece over and press it again, making sure there are no puckers.

b. Repeat step 3a to fuse the interfacing pieces to one pocket panel and all four bands. The main panel interfacings will be attached in steps 4c and 4h.

4

PLEAT THE EXTERIOR AND MAKE THE MAIN PANELS.

a. Place the exterior fabric for the pleated panel on the ironing board, **Right** side up. Measure 1" (2.5 cm) up from one short edge and make a parallel mark on each long side edge. These marks will be used as a guide to form the first pleat only. Pinch ½" (1.3 cm) of the fabric above the 1" (2.5 cm) marks on each side edge and fold it toward the marks. Press the pleat that forms on the **Right** side of the fabric flat, being careful to keep the pleat even across the width of the fabric. Continue to pinch the fabric above the previous pleat and fold back toward the pleat you just pressed. Vary the pleat widths between ³⁄₈" (1 cm) and ⁵⁄₈" (1.6 cm). Press each pleat as it is formed, creating a nice crisp edge.

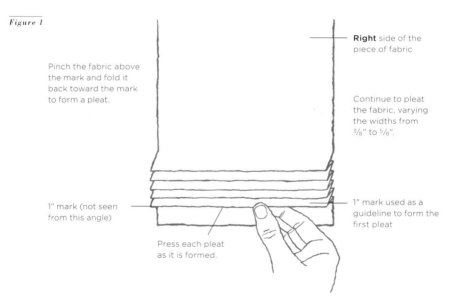

Figure 1

Pinch the fabric above the mark and fold it back toward the mark to form a pleat.

Right side of the piece of fabric

Continue to pleat the fabric, varying the widths from ³⁄₈" to ⁵⁄₈".

1" mark (not seen from this angle)

1" mark used as a guideline to form the first pleat

Press each pleat as it is formed.

b. Gently turn the pleated fabric **Wrong** side up, placing the pleats vertically. Adjust the pleats if necessary.

c. Center the fusible side of one of the main panel interfacing pieces onto the **Wrong** side of the pleated fabric. Make sure the pleats are straight and even. Using a damp pressing cloth, fuse the interfacing in place.

d. Machine baste* a ¼" (0.6 cm) seam completely around the outside edges on the interfaced side of the panel.

e. Using a ruler and fabric marker, measure down from the top at each side edge of the interfacing main panel and mark the following measurements for the size clutch you are making.
For small clutch: 1½" (3.8 cm) and then 5" (2.7 cm)
For medium clutch: 2" (5.1 cm) and then 5½" (14 cm)
For large clutch: 2½" (6.4 cm) and then 6" (15.2 cm)

Connect the first two marks by drawing a horizontal line across the main panel. Then connect the second set of marks with a horizontal line.

f. Stitch following the marked lines and backstitch* at each end. Be careful to keep the pleats flat as you sew.

g. With your scissors, cut away the excess pleated fabric, using the outside edges of the interfacing main panel as a cutting guide.

h. Repeat steps 4a through 4g to make the second main panel.

5 **MAKE AND ATTACH THE HANDLE.**

a. Place the handles **Right** sides together, matching the long side edges, and pin them in place. Stitch a ½" (1.3 cm) seam along each pinned edge. Backstitch at each end.

b. Clip* in the seam allowance* along the curve at the center of the handle, being careful not to clip your stitching. Turn the handle **Right** side out through one open end and press it flat. Then, edge stitch* along the finished edges.

c. Find the center of one main panel by folding it in half and marking the top edge of the fold with a straight pin. Then, open the main panel.

d. Fold the handle in half, matching the short raw ends, and pin. Center the matched raw ends at the center top edge on the **Right** side of one of the main panels, and pin. Machine baste a ¼" (0.6 cm) seam across the edges to hold the handle in place.

Please set the handle/main panels aside for now.

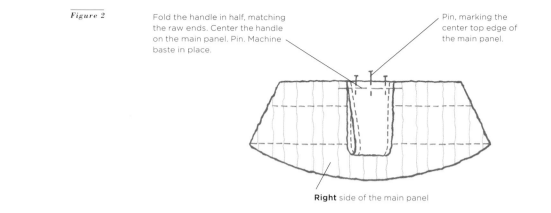

Figure 2

Fold the handle in half, matching the raw ends. Center the handle on the main panel. Pin. Machine baste in place.

Pin, marking the center top edge of the main panel.

Right side of the main panel

6   MAKE AND ATTACH THE POCKET TO THE LINING.

a. Place the pocket panels **Right** sides together, matching all edges. Pin along the top edge. Stitch a ½" (1.3 cm) seam across the pinned edge. Backstitch at each end.

b. Turn the pocket panels **Right** side out and press the seam at the top edge. Then, topstitch* ¼" (0.6 cm) from the finished edge. Backstitch at each end.

c. Match the side and bottom edges and pin. Machine baste a ¼" (0.6 cm) seam to hold the pinned edges together.

d. Place the pocket on one of the lining main panels, matching the bottom and side edges, and pin. Machine baste a ¼" (0.6 cm) seam to hold the pocket in place.

e. Fold the lining and pocket panels in half, matching the side edges, and gently press a center crease on the fold. Stitch up along the crease to divide the pocket into two sections. Backstitch at each end.

7   PREPARE AND ATTACH THE BANDS TO THE EXTERIOR AND LINING.

a. Place the bottom edge of one exterior band and the top edge of one pleated main panel **Right** sides together, matching the edges, and pin in place. Stitch a ½" (1.3 cm) seam across the pinned edge. Backstitch at each end.

b. Press the seam allowance toward the band. Then, topstitch ¼" (0.6 cm) from the seam on the **Right** side of the band.

c. Repeat steps 7a and 7b to attach the other exterior band to the second exterior main panel and both lining bands to the lining main panels.

8

INSTALL THE ZIPPER.

a. Place the zipper face down onto the **Right** side of the first exterior panel with the zipper head ½" (1.3 cm) from one side raw edge of the band. Place the long edge of the zipper tape ¼" (0.6 cm) from the top edge of the band and pin it in place.

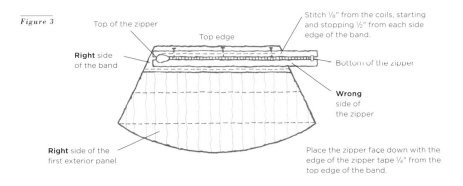

Figure 3

Top of the zipper

Top edge

Stitch ⅛" from the coils, starting and stopping ½" from each side edge of the band.

Right side of the band

Bottom of the zipper

Wrong side of the zipper

Right side of the first exterior panel

Place the zipper face down with the edge of the zipper tape ¼" from the top edge of the band.

b. Using the zipper foot for your machine, stitch ⅛" (0.3 cm) from the zipper coils, starting and stopping ½" (1.3 cm) from each side edge. Backstitch at each end.

c. Place the first lining panel **Right** sides together with the exterior panel, sandwiching the zipper in between. Pin them in place along the top edge.

d. With the *interfaced* side of the exterior panel facing up, sew over the stitching that attached the zipper, starting and stopping ½" (1.3 cm) from each side edge of the band. Backstitch at each end.

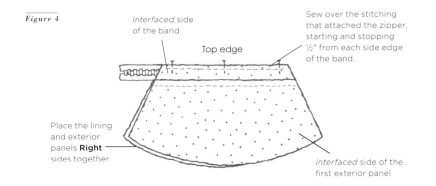

Figure 4

Interfaced side of the band

Top edge

Sew over the stitching that attached the zipper, starting and stopping ½" from each side edge of the band.

Place the lining and exterior panels **Right** sides together

Interfaced side of the first exterior panel

e. Flip the lining over the zipper, matching the **Wrong** sides of the lining and the exterior panels. Pin them together. Press the panels away from the zipper, pressing under the ½" (1.3 cm) unstitched fabric at each end.

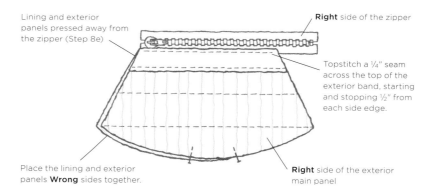

Figure 5

Lining and exterior panels pressed away from the zipper (Step 8e)

Right side of the zipper

Topstitch a ¼" seam across the top of the exterior band, starting and stopping ½" from each side edge.

Place the lining and exterior panels **Wrong** sides together.

Right side of the exterior main panel

f. On the **Right** side of the exterior, starting and stopping ½" (1.3 cm) from each side edge, topstitch ¼" (0.6 cm) from the seam that attached the zipper to the exterior band. Backstitch at each end.

g. Repeat steps 8a through 8f to attach the other exterior and lining panels to the other side of the zipper. Be careful not to twist the zipper.

h. With the exterior panels facing up, lay the panels with the zipper attached on a flat surface, spreading each set of exterior and lining panels away from the zipper. Measure ½" (1.3 cm) in from the side edge of the panels along the bottom of the zipper and make a mark on the zipper coils. Bar tack* over the coils to make a new zipper stop.

i. Trim the excess zipper, leaving a 1" (2.5 cm) tail beyond the new zipper stop.

j. Open the zipper and remove the pins from the panels.

9   ATTACH THE EXTERIOR AND LINING PANELS.

Note: Leave the zipper halfway open for this step so you can turn the bag Right side out.

a. Separate the exterior panels from the lining panels. To keep the lining out of your way while you stitch the exterior panels, place the lining panels **Right** sides together, matching the raw edges, and pin them in place. Then, fold the unstitched edges at the top of the lining bands in toward the center of the panel and pin them in place. (See Figure 6.)

b. Place the exterior panels **Right** sides together, matching the seams attaching the bands, the side and bottom edges, and the unstitched top edges. Pin them together. Starting and stopping at the top folded edge, stitch a ½" (1.3 cm) seam down both sides and across the bottom edges. Backstitch at each end.

c. Trim* all four corners in the seam allowances, being careful not to clip your stitching. Press the seam allowances open.

Figure 6

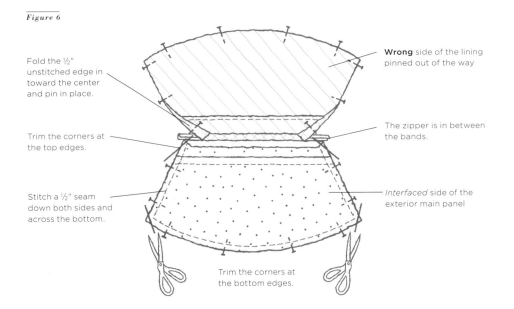

Fold the ½" unstitched edge in toward the center and pin in place.

Trim the corners at the top edges.

Stitch a ½" seam down both sides and across the bottom.

Wrong side of the lining pinned out of the way

The zipper is in between the bands.

Interfaced side of the exterior main panel

Trim the corners at the bottom edges.

d. Unpin the lining panels at each end of the zipper. Place these edges **Right** sides together, matching the seams that attach the bands. Pin them together. Starting and stopping just under the zipper teeth, stitch a ½" (1.3 cm) seam down both sides and across the bottom edges. Leave a 4" (10.2 cm) opening centered at the bottom edge for turning the bag **Right** side out. Back-stitch at each end.

e. Repeat step 9c to trim the corners and press.

10 COMPLETE THE BAG.

a. Turn the bag **Right** side out through the opening in the bottom of the lining.

b. Fold each side of the opening under ½" (1.3 cm) toward the **Wrong** side, and press. Pin the edges together and edge stitch the opening closed. Then, push the lining down inside the exterior. Use a turning tool* to gently push out the corners.

c. Pin the exterior and lining bands together at the center of each main panel. Following the topstitching already in place on the band, stitch 1½" (3.8 cm) across the center to hold the lining in place. Backstitch at each end.

Your Clutch is complete! As easy as this purse was to make, you'll have even more fun collecting compliments over the elegant details—remember, mum's the word. Don't tell your friends how easily you created your purse. Let them have some fun and find out for themselves!

06

Teardrop Bag

Accented with a beautiful central pleat and eye-catching "hipped" shoulder straps, this hip bag will turn heads. The smaller size is perfect for ladies on the go or as a wallet and keys stash. The larger size is a cool daily runaround bag for school, market, or errands. Whip up several bags in fabrics from funky to fabulous and start your own trend.

FINISHED SIZES	**Small bag**
	9½" (24.1 cm) wide x 9" (22.9 cm) tall [18½" (47 cm) with handles]
	Large bag
	13½" (34.3 cm) wide x 11¾" (29.8 cm) tall [29½" (75 cm) with handles]

- -

FABRICS

From 44" (112 cm) wide light- to mid-weight fabric

- $3/8$ yd (0.34 m) of one print for the exterior main panels

- $5/8$ yd (0.57 m) of a coordinating print for the exterior bands, handles, and handle extensions (referred to as "hip" below)

- $1/2$ yd (0.46 m) of a second coordinating print for the lining

- -

OTHER SUPPLIES

- $1½$ yd (1.37 m) of 20" (50.8 cm) wide fusible woven interfacing (I use Shape Flex SF-101 by Pellon)

- One $1/2$" (1.3 cm) magnetic snap (I use Prym-Dritz brand)

- 1 small spool coordinating all-purpose thread (I use Coats Dual Duty XP)

See Basic Tools Needed for Each Project (page 14).

- -

ADDITIONAL TOOL NEEDED

- Safety pin

Follow these instructions to make either size bag. Any measurement changes will be noted in the specific step.

1 CUT OUT THE PATTERN PIECES.

From the pattern sheet included with this book, cut out:
- Main/pocket panel
- Handle
- Hip (used as a handle extension)

2 CUT OUT ALL OF THE PIECES FROM THE FABRIC.

a. Fold the exterior and lining fabrics in half lengthwise, **Wrong** sides together, matching the selvage edges.* Gently press a crease on the fold. Open the fabric and fold each selvage edge in to meet the center crease. This will give you enough folded edges to cut out the exterior main panels and lining.

From the first exterior print fabric
- Cut 2 main panels on the fold*

From the coordinating exterior fabric
b. Fold the fabric in half lengthwise, with **Wrong** sides together, matching the selvage edges.
- Cut 2 handles on the fold
- Cut 4 hips on the fold

c. Using a ruler and fabric marker, measure and mark the dimensions below directly on the **Right** side of the fabric. Then, cut along the marked lines.

- Cut 4 bands for small bag: $2\frac{1}{4}$" (5.7 cm) wide x $8\frac{1}{2}$" (21.6 cm) long

OR

- Cut 4 bands for large bag: $2\frac{3}{4}$" (7 cm) wide x 12" (30.5 cm) long

From the lining fabric
- Cut 2 main panels on the fold
- Cut 2 pocket panels on the fold. Fold the main panel pattern piece back at the dashed lines.

From the fusible interfacing
d. Use the panels you have cut as full-size pattern pieces to cut out the fusible interfacing.
- Cut 2 main panels
- Cut 2 handles
- Cut 1 pocket panel
- Cut 4 bands

3

APPLY THE FUSIBLE INTERFACING.

Note: See page 172 for interfacing application tips.

a. Place the **Wrong** side of the first exterior main panel onto the fusible side of one coordinating interfacing. Using a damp pressing cloth,* fuse the interfacing in place. Turn the panels over and press them again, making sure there are no puckers.

b. Repeat step 3a to fuse the coordinating interfacing to the second exterior main panel, all four bands, both handles, and one pocket panel.

4

PLEAT THE EXTERIOR MAIN PANELS.

a. Fold the first exterior main panel in half, **Right** sides together, matching the side edges. Gently press a crease on the fold at the top edge only. Pin the top edges together.

b. Stitch a seam along the folded edge; 1" (2.5 cm) in for the small bag or 1½" (3.8 cm) in for the large. Sew 1½" (3.8 cm) in length down from the top raw edge of the panel, and backstitch* at each end. *Note: Figure 1 shows the small bag.*

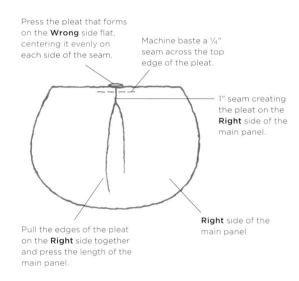

Figure 1

Press the pleat that forms on the **Wrong** side flat, centering it evenly on each side of the seam.

Machine baste a ¼" seam across the top edge of the pleat.

1" seam creating the pleat on the **Right** side of the main panel.

c. Open the panel. Press the pleat that forms on the **Wrong** side of the fabric flat, centering the fabric evenly over the stitching line. Pin and then machine baste* ¼" (0.6 cm) from the top edge of the pleat to hold it in place.

Pull the edges of the pleat on the **Right** side together and press the length of the main panel.

Right side of the main panel

d. Press the pleat on the **Right** side of the main panel the full length of the panel. This will give the bag its shape.

e. Repeat steps 4a through 4d to make a pleat on the other exterior main panel.

5

ATTACH THE BANDS TO THE EXTERIOR MAIN PANELS.

a. With **Right** sides together, match the top edge of the main panel to one long edge of the band and pin in place. Stitch a ½" (1.3 cm) seam across the pinned edge. Backstitch at each end.

b. Press the seam allowance* toward the band. Then, edge stitch* across the band just above the seam.

c. Repeat steps 5a and 5b to attach the other exterior band and main panel.

6   MAKE THE EXTERIOR OF THE BAG.

a. Place the exterior panels **Right** sides together, matching the side and bottom edges and the seams that attach the bands. Pin all matched edges and seams together.

b. Stitch a ½" (1.3 cm) seam along the pinned edges, pivoting at each seam. Backstitch at each end.

c. Clip* into the seam allowance at the seams where you pivoted, being careful not to clip your stitching. Trim* the seam allowance to ¼" (0.6 cm) on the curved edges below the clips. Press the side seam allowance on the band open.

d. Turn the exterior **Right** side out and use a turning tool* to gently round out the edges. Press the exterior.

7   MAKE AND ATTACH THE HIPS.

a. Place two hip pieces **Right** sides together matching all the edges, and pin in place. Stitch a ½" (1.3 cm) seam around the pinned edges. Backstitch at each end.

b. Trim the seam allowance to ¼" (0.6 cm). Clip into the seam allowance every ½" (1.3 cm) around the curved edge, being careful not to clip your stitching.

c. Turn the hip **Right** side out and use a turning tool to gently round out the edges. Press it flat.

d. Fold the hip in half, matching the side edges, and gently press a crease on the fold. Open the hip.

e. Place the exterior of the bag with one of the side seams facing up. Center the crease on the hip over the side seam, matching the top edges, and pin in place.

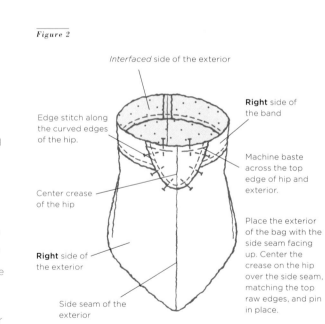

Figure 2

Interfaced side of the exterior

Edge stitch along the curved edges of the hip.

Center crease of the hip

Right side of the exterior

Side seam of the exterior

Right side of the band

Machine baste across the top edge of hip and exterior.

Place the exterior of the bag with the side seam facing up. Center the crease on the hip over the side seam, matching the top raw edges, and pin in place.

f. Edge stitch along the curved edges of the hip. Backstitch at each end. Then, machine baste a ¼" (0.6 cm) seam across the top edge.

g. Repeat steps 7a through 7f to make and attach the other hip to the opposite side of the exterior.

8 **MAKE AND ATTACH THE HANDLE.**

a. Place the two handles **Right** sides together, matching the long edges, and pin in place.

b. Stitch a ½" (1.3 cm) seam along the pinned edges, leaving a 6" (15.2 cm) opening centered on one side of the handle for turning it **Right** side out. Backstitch at each end.

c. Clip into the seam allowances every ½" to ¾" (1.3 cm to 1.9 cm) at the curves on both ends of the handle, being careful not to clip your stitching.

d. Attach a safety pin to a single layer of the handle at one end. Using the safety pin as a guide, push the pin through the end of the handle and out the center opening. Then, move the pin to the other end and repeat the process to turn the remainder of the handle **Right** side out. Remove the safety pin.

Figure 3

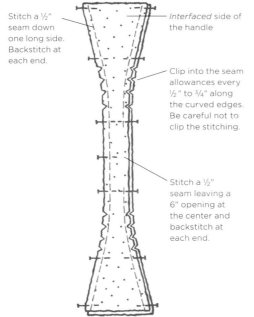

Place the handles **Right** sides together, matching the long edges, and pin in place.

Stitch a ½" seam down one long side. Backstitch at each end.

Interfaced side of the handle

Clip into the seam allowances every ½" to ¾" along the curved edges. Be careful not to clip the stitching.

Stitch a ½" seam leaving a 6" opening at the center and backstitch at each end.

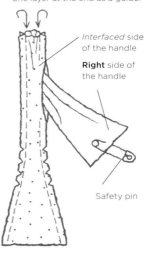

Turn the handle **Right** side out, using a safety pin attached to one layer at the end as a guide.

Interfaced side of the handle

Right side of the handle

Safety pin

e. Use a turning tool to gently push out the edges and press the handle flat. Fold each side of the opening under ½" (1.3 cm) toward the **Wrong** side, and press. Pin the edges together.

f. Edge stitch down both long sides of the handle. This will close the opening and give the handle a smooth finish.

g. Fold the wide ends of the handle in half across the width and gently press a crease on each fold.

h. Place one end of the handle on the left side edge of the exterior, matching the crease on the handle to the crease on the hip, and the ends of the handle to the top edges of the exterior band. Pin in place.

i. Place the other end of the handle on the right side of the exterior, matching the creases and edges. Be careful not to twist the handle. Pin in place. Then, machine baste a ¼" (0.6 cm) seam across both pinned ends.

9 PLEAT THE LINING MAIN PANELS.

a. Fold the first lining main panel in half, **Right** sides together, matching the side edges. Gently press a crease on the fold at the top and bottom of the panel. Pin along the folded edges.

b. Repeat steps 4b and 4c to make a 1" (2.5 cm) pleat. Make this pleat at both the top and the bottom edges of the panel. Press the pleats flat, centering the fabric evenly over the stitching lines.

c. Repeat steps 9a and 9b to pleat the second lining main panel.

10 MAKE AND ATTACH THE POCKET TO THE LINING MAIN PANEL.

a. Place the pocket panels **Right** sides together, matching the edges. Pin along the top edge. Stitch a ½" (1.3 cm) seam across the pinned edge. Backstitch at each end.

b. Turn the pocket panels **Right** side out and press along the top edge. Then topstitch* ¼" (0.6 cm) from this edge. Backstitch at each end.

c. Match the outer curved edges of the pocket panel and pin. Machine baste a ¼" (0.6 cm) seam across the pinned edges.

d. Place the pocket onto the **Right** side of one lining main panel, matching the outer and curved edges, and pin in place. Machine baste a ¼" (0.6 cm) seam to hold the pocket in place.

11 INSTALL THE MAGNETIC SNAP ON THE LINING BANDS.

a. Fold one lining band in half, matching the short ends, and gently press a crease on the fold.

b. Open the band. Refold it, matching the long edges, and gently press a crease on the fold.

c. Open the band again. On the **Right** side, center the male half of the magnetic snap over the point where the creases cross. Follow the manufacturer's instructions to install the snap.

d. Repeat steps 11a through 11c to install the female half of the snap on the second lining band.

12 ATTACH THE BANDS AND COMPLETE THE LINING.

a. Repeat step 5 to attach the lining bands to the lining main panels.

b. Repeat steps 6a through 6c to attach the lining panels, leaving a 4" (10.2 cm) opening centered at the bottom for turning the bag **Right** side out. Leave the lining **Wrong** side out.

13 ATTACH THE EXTERIOR AND LINING TO COMPLETE THE BAG.

a. With the exterior **Right** side out and the lining **Wrong** side out, slide the lining over the exterior, tucking the handle down between the two layers.

b. Match the top edges, side seams, and handle edges and pin in place. Stitch a ½" (1.3 cm) seam completely around the top edges. Backstitch at each end.

c. Turn the bag **Right** side out by pulling it through the opening on the bottom of the lining. Push the lining down inside the exterior, pulling out the handle.

d. Press the top edge and pin. Edge stitch completely around the top edge and backstitch at each end.

e. Pin the exterior and lining bands together at the center of each main panel. Follow the previous edge stitching on the band and sew 1½" (3.8 cm) across the center to secure the lining. Backstitch at each end.

f. Pull the bottom of the lining out of the bag. Fold each side of the opening under ½" (1.3 cm) toward the **Wrong** side, and press. Pin and then edge stitch to close the opening. Backstitch at each end. Push the lining back down inside the bag. Press.

Your Teardrop Bag is complete! Take it with you for a fun night out, a quick day trip, or anything in between. Go forth and flaunt your personal style!

PROJECT:

07

TITLE:

Key Keeper Coin Purse

This little nugget is a great add-on for the Teardrop Bag (page 79) or a stand-alone purse to keep or gift. With a key tab and an adorable pleat, it will become your new best friend. Think cell phone holder, makeup bag, cash stash, or buttons and beads bag. Or, do what I do and make one to use for each purpose!

FINISHED SIZE	5³/₄" (14.6 cm) wide x 5¹/₂" (14 cm) tall

===

FABRICS	**From 44" (112 cm) wide light- to mid-weight fabric** • ¹/₄ yd (0.23 m) of one print for the exterior main panels • ¹/₈ yd (0.11 m) of a coordinating print for the exterior bands and tab • ³/₈ yd (0.34 m) of a second coordinating print for the lining

- -

OTHER SUPPLIES	• ³/₈ yd (0.34 m) of 20" (50.8 cm) wide fusible woven interfacing (I use Shape Flex SF-101 by Pellon) • One 7" (17.9 cm) coordinating zipper (I use Coats brand) • 1 small spool coordinating all-purpose thread (I use Coats Dual Duty XP) *See Basic Tools Needed for Each Project (page 14).*

- -

ADDITIONAL TOOL NEEDED	• Zipper foot for your sewing machine

1 CUT OUT THE PATTERN PIECES.

From the pattern sheet included with this book, cut out

• Main panel
• Pocket panel

2 CUT OUT ALL OF THE PIECES FROM THE FABRIC.

a. Fold the first exterior print and lining fabrics in half lengthwise, **Wrong** sides together, matching the selvage edges.* Gently press a crease on each of the folded edges. Open the fabrics. Fold each selvage edge in 5" (12.7 cm) toward the **Wrong** side. This will give you enough folded edges to cut out the main panels and pocket panels.

From the first exterior print fabric

• Cut 2 main panels on the fold*

From the coordinating exterior fabric

b. Using a ruler and fabric marker, measure and mark these dimensions directly onto the **Right** side of a single layer of fabric. Then, cut along the marked lines.

• Cut 2 bands: 5½" (14 cm) wide x 2" (5.1 cm) long
• Cut 1 tab: 2" (5.1 cm) wide x 2½" (6.4 cm) long

From the lining fabric

• Cut 2 main panels on the fold
• Cut 2 pocket panels on the fold

c. Open the fabric. Measure and mark these dimensions directly on the **Right** side of a single layer of fabric. Then, cut along the marked lines.

• Cut 2 bands: 5½" (14 cm) wide x 2" (5.1 cm) long

From the fusible interfacing

d. Use the panels you have cut out as full-size pattern pieces to cut the interfacing on a single layer.

• Cut 2 main panels
• Cut 1 pocket panel
• Cut 2 bands

3 APPLY THE FUSIBLE INTERFACING.

Note: See page 172 for interfacing application tips.

a. Place the **Wrong** side of the first exterior main panel onto the fusible side of the corresponding interfacing panel. Using a damp pressing cloth,* fuse the interfacing in place. Turn the panels over and press them again, making sure there are no puckers.

b. Repeat step 3a to fuse the interfacing to the second exterior main panel, both exterior bands, and one pocket panel.

4 PLEAT THE EXTERIOR MAIN PANELS.

a. Fold the first exterior main panel in half, **Right** sides together, matching the side raw edges. Gently press a crease on the fold along the top of the finished edge only. Pin the top edges together.

b. Stitch ½" (1.3 cm) from the folded edge, 1" (2.5 cm) in length down from the top edge of the panel, and backstitch* at each end.

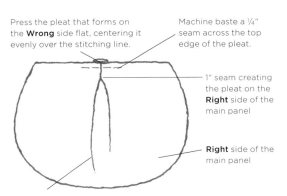

Figure 1

Press the pleat that forms on the **Wrong** side flat, centering it evenly over the stitching line.

Machine baste a ¼" seam across the top edge of the pleat.

1" seam creating the pleat on the **Right** side of the main panel

Right side of the main panel

Pull the edges of the pleat on the **Right** side together and press the length of the main panel.

c. Open the panel. Press the pleat that forms on the **Wrong** side of the fabric flat, centering it evenly over the stitching line. Pin and then machine baste* a ¼" (0.6 cm) seam across the top edge of the pleat to hold it in place.

d. Press the pleat on the **Right** side of the main panel the full length of the panel. This will give the bag its shape.

e. Repeat steps 4a through 4d to make a top center pleat on the other exterior main panel.

5 ATTACH THE BANDS TO THE EXTERIOR MAIN PANELS.

a. Place one exterior band and exterior main panel **Right** sides together, matching the top edge of the main panel to one long edge of the band, and pin in place. Stitch a ½" (1.3 cm) seam across the pinned edge. Backstitch at each end.

b. Press the seam allowance* toward the band. Then, edge stitch* the band just above the seam.

c. Repeat steps 5a and 5b to attach the other exterior band to the second exterior main panel.

6 PLEAT THE LINING MAIN PANELS.

a. Fold the first lining main panel in half, **Right** sides together, matching the side edges. Gently press a crease on the fold along the top and bottom edges. Pin the edges in place.

b. Repeat steps 4b and 4c to make a pleat on both the top *and* the bottom edges. Press the pleats flat, centering the fabric evenly over the stitching line.

c. Repeat steps 6a and 6b to pleat the second lining main panel.

7 ATTACH THE LINING BANDS TO THE LINING MAIN PANELS.

Repeat step 5 to attach the lining bands to the lining main panels.

8

MAKE AND ATTACH THE POCKET TO THE LINING.

a. Place the pocket panels **Right** sides together, matching all of the edges. Pin along the top edge. Stitch a ½" (1.3 cm) seam across the pinned edge. Backstitch at each end.

b. Turn the pocket **Right** side out and press along the top edge. Then, topstitch ¼" (0.6 cm) from the edge. Backstitch at each end.

c. Match the outer curved edges and pin all around the panels. Machine baste ¼" (0.6 cm) from the pinned edges.

d. Place the pocket onto the **Right** side of one lining main panel, matching the bottom and side edges, and pin in place. Machine baste ¼" (0.6 cm) from the edge of the pocket.

9

INSTALL THE ZIPPER.

a. Place the zipper face down onto the **Right** side of the first exterior panel with the zipper head ½" (1.3 cm) from the side edge of the band. Place the long edge of the zipper tape ¼" (0.6 cm) from the top edge of the band and pin it in place.

b. Using the zipper foot for your machine, stitch ⅛" (0.3 cm) from the zipper coils, starting and stopping ½" (1.3 cm) from each side edge. Backstitch at each end.

c. Place the first lining panel **Right** sides together with the exterior panel, sandwiching the zipper in between. Pin them in place along the top edge.

d. With the *interfaced* side of the exterior panel facing up, sew over the stitching that attached the zipper, starting and stopping ½" (1.3 cm) from each side edge. Backstitch at each end.

e. Flip the lining over the zipper, matching the **Wrong** sides of each panel. Pin them together. Press the panels away from the zipper. pressing under the ½" (1.3 cm) unstitched fabric at each end.

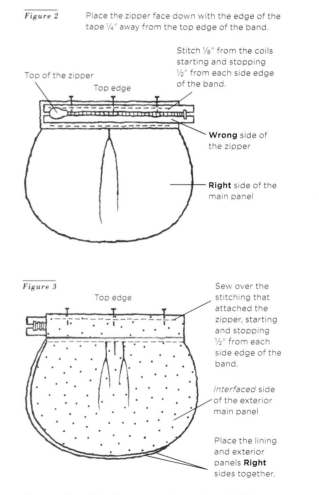

Figure 2 — Place the zipper face down with the edge of the tape ¼" away from the top edge of the band.

Stitch ⅛" from the coils starting and stopping ½" from each side edge of the band.

Top of the zipper

Top edge

Wrong side of the zipper

Right side of the main panel

Figure 3

Top edge

Sew over the stitching that attached the zipper, starting and stopping ½" from each side edge of the band.

Interfaced side of the exterior main panel

Place the lining and exterior panels **Right** sides together.

f. On the **Right** side of the exterior, topstitch a ¼" (0.6 cm) seam across the top of the exterior band, starting and stopping ½" (1.3 cm) from each side edge. Backstitch at each end.

g. Repeat steps 9a through 9f to attach the second exterior and lining panels to the other side of the zipper.

h. With the exterior panels facing up, lay the panels on a flat surface, spreading each set of exterior and lining panels away from the zipper. Measure ½" (1.3 cm) in from the side edges along the bottom of the zipper and make a mark on the zipper coils. Bar tack* over the coils to make a new zipper stop.

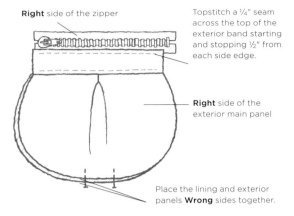

Figure 4

Right side of the zipper

Topstitch a ¼" seam across the top of the exterior band starting and stopping ½" from each side edge.

Right side of the exterior main panel

Place the lining and exterior panels **Wrong** sides together.

i. Use your scissors to trim the excess zipper, leaving a 1" (2.5 cm) tail beyond the new zipper stop. Open the zipper and remove the pins from the panels.

10 MAKE AND ATTACH THE TAB TO ONE EXTERIOR MAIN PANEL.

a. Fold the tab in half, **Wrong** sides together, matching the short ends. Press a crease along the folded edge.

b. Open the tab and fold each side in to meet the center crease, and press.

c. Fold the tab in half again at the center crease to enclose the raw edges, and press. Pin the folded edges.

d. Edge stitch down the folded edges and backstitch at each end.

e. Fold the tab in half, matching the short ends, and pin.

f. On the **Right** side of one of the exterior main panels, measure and mark 1¼" (3.2 cm) down from the top edge of the band at the end with the top of the zipper.

g. Place the pinned ends of the tab even with the side edge of the exterior main panel just below the mark, and pin in place. Machine baste a ¼" (0.6 cm) seam to secure the tab.

11 ATTACH THE EXTERIOR AND LINING PANELS.

Note: Leave the zipper open for this step so you can turn the bag Right side out.

a. Separate the exterior from the lining panels. To keep the lining out of your way while you stitch the exterior panels, place the lining panels **Right** sides together, matching the raw edges, and pin them in place. Then, fold the unstitched edges at the top of the lining bands in toward the center and pin in place.

b. Place the exterior panels **Right** sides together, matching the edges and the seam that attaches the bands. Pin in place. Starting and stopping at the top folded edge on each end of the zipper, stitch a ½" (1.3 cm) seam down each side. Pivot at the seam on the band and around the curve of the main panel. Backstitch at each end.

c. Trim* the top corners in the seam allowances at the top edges of the exterior panels, making sure not to clip your stitching.

d. Clip* into the seam allowance at the seam that attaches the band to the main panel, being careful not to clip your stitching. Trim the seam allowance to ¼" (0.6 cm) along the curved edge below the clip. Press the side seam allowance on the band open.

e. Then, unpin the unstitched top corners of the lining panel.

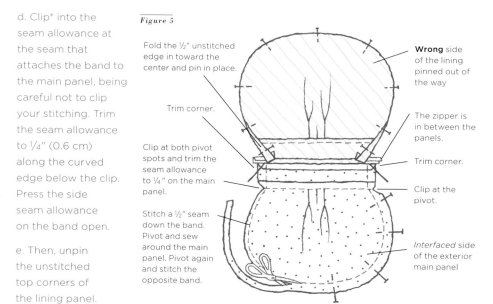

Figure 5

Fold the ½" unstitched edge in toward the center and pin in place.

Trim corner.

Clip at both pivot spots and trim the seam allowance to ¼" on the main panel.

Stitch a ½" seam down the band. Pivot and sew around the main panel. Pivot again and stitch the opposite band.

Wrong side of the lining pinned out of the way

The zipper is in between the panels.

Trim corner.

Clip at the pivot.

Interfaced side of the exterior main panel

f. Repeat steps 11b through 11d to attach the lining panels, leaving a 4" (10.2 cm) opening centered on the bottom for turning the bag **Right** side out.

12 **COMPLETE THE BAG.**

a. Turn the bag **Right** side out through the opening in the bottom of the lining.

b. Keep the bottom of the lining outside of the exterior bag. Fold each side of the opening under ½" (1.3 cm) toward the **Wrong** side, and press. Pin the edges together and then edge stitch the opening closed. Backstitch at each end.

c. Push the lining down inside the exterior. Use a turning tool* to gently push out the curves.

d. Smooth the lining and exterior bands at the top open end of the zipper and pin them together. Topstitch across the side seam over the current edge stitching. This will secure the lining. Backstitch at each end.

Your Coin Purse is complete! Now you can keep your keys, coins, and other essentials on hand and pretty in plain sight!

08

Fringed Hobo Bag

If you're looking to run away from home (read: sneak off for a latte or to the mall), then do it properly and take along your very own (stylish!) Fringed Hobo Bag. This bag sports a jazzy, rounded style in two sizes, with a longer strap on the regular size and a shorter strap on the larger size. Accent it with sassy tassel trim that travels the circumference of the bag. Stash everything you need for your adventure in the large compartment, and hit the road.

FINISHED SIZE	**Small bag** 17 1/2" (44.5 cm) wide x 11" (27.9 cm) tall [26 1/4" (66.8 cm) tall with handles] x 2 1/2" (6.4 cm) deep **Large bag** 19 3/4" (50.2 cm) wide x 14" (35.6 cm) tall [24" (61 cm) tall with handles] x 2 1/2" (6.4 cm) deep

= =

FABRICS	**From 44" (112 cm) wide light- to mid-weight fabric OR 54" (137 cm) wide mid-weight Home Dec fabric** **For the small bag:** • 1 1/8 yd (1.03 m) of one print for the exterior • 7/8 yd (0.8 m) of a coordinating print for the yoke • 1 5/8 yd (1.49 m) of a second coordinating print for the lining **For the large bag:** • 1 3/8 yd (1.26 m) of one print for the exterior • 7/8 yd (0.8 m) of a coordinating print for the yoke • 1 5/8 yd (1.49 m) of a second coordinating print for the lining

— —

OTHER SUPPLIES	**For the small bag:** **If using light- to mid-weight fabric** • 3 3/8 yd (3.09 m) of 20" (50.8 cm) wide fusible woven interfacing (I use Shape Flex SF-101 by Pellon) • 2 yd (1.83 m) of 44" (112 cm) wide fusible fleece (I use fusible Thermolam Plus by Pellon) **If using a mid-weight Home Dec fabric** • 2 7/8 yd (2.63 m) of 20" (50.8 cm) wide fusible woven interfacing (I use Shape Flex SF-101 by Pellon) • 1 yd (0.91 m) of 44" (112 cm) wide fusible fleece (I use fusible Thermolam Plus by Pellon) **Plus for either weight fabric** • 2 3/4 yd (2.51 m) of 1" (2.5 cm) to 1 1/2" (3.8 cm) long tassel trim • 1 spool coordinating all-purpose thread (I use Coats Dual Duty XP)

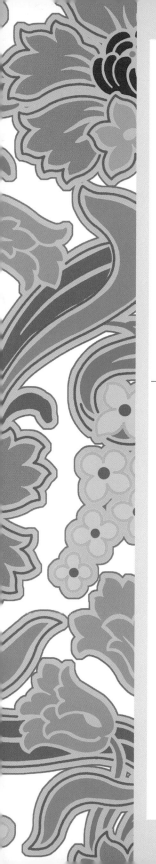

OTHER SUPPLIES

For the large bag:

If using a light- to mid-weight fabric

• 3¾ yd (3.43 m) of 20" (50.8 cm) wide fusible woven interfacing (I use Shape Flex SF-101 by Pellon)
• 2½ yd (2.29 m) of 44" (112 cm) wide fusible fleece (I use fusible Thermolam Plus by Pellon)

If using a mid-weight Home Dec fabric

• 3¼ yd (2.97 m) of 20" (50.8 cm) wide fusible woven interfacing (I use Shape Flex SF-101 by Pellon)
• 1¼ yd (1.14 m) of 44" (112 cm) wide fusible fleece (I use fusible Thermolam Plus by Pellon)

Plus for either weight fabric

• 3¼ yd (2.97 m) of 1" (2.5 cm) to 1½" (3.8 cm) long tassel trim
• 1 spool coordinating all-purpose thread (I use Coats Dual Duty XP)

See Basic Tools Needed for Each Project (page 14).

ADDITIONAL TOOLS NEEDED

• Tracing wheel
• Wax-free tracing paper (I use Prym-Dritz brand)
• Zipper foot for your sewing machine

Follow these instructions to make the shoulder bag with a long handle and the large bag with a short handle.

1 CUT OUT THE PATTERN PIECES.

From the pattern sheet included with this book, cut out

- Main panel
- Inside pocket panel
- Yoke

2 CUT OUT ALL OF THE PIECES FROM THE FABRIC.

a. Fold each of the fabrics in half lengthwise **Wrong** sides together, matching the selvage edges,* and gently press a crease. Open the fabric. Fold each edge in to meet the crease with **Wrong** sides together. This will give you enough folded edges to cut out the panels.

From the print exterior fabric

- Cut 2 main panels on the fold*

b. Open the fabric. Using a ruler and fabric marker, measure and mark the dimensions directly onto the **Right** side of a single layer of fabric. Then, cut along the marked lines.

- Cut 2 side panels: $3^{1}/_{2}$" (8.9 cm) wide x 36" (91.4 cm) long

Note: The side panel is used to make the sides and bottom of the bag, as well as the handle.

From the coordinating exterior fabric

- Cut 2 yokes on the fold

From the lining fabric

- Cut 2 main panels on the fold
- Cut 4 inside pocket panels on the fold

c. Open the fabric. Measure and mark the dimensions directly onto the **Right** side of a single layer of fabric. Then, cut along the marked lines.

- Cut 2 side panels: $3^{1}/_{2}$" (8.9 cm) wide x 36" (91.4 cm) long

d. Use the panels you have cut as full-size pattern pieces to cut out the fusible interfacing and fleece.

From the fusible interfacing

If using light- to mid-weight fabric

- Cut 4 main panels
- Cut 2 yokes
- Cut 4 side panels
- Cut 4 inside pocket panels

If using mid-weight Home Dec fabric
- Cut 4 main panels
- Cut 2 yokes
- Cut 2 side panels
- Cut 2 inside pocket panels

From the fusible fleece

If using light- to mid-weight fabric
- Cut 4 main panels
- Cut 4 side panels

If using mid-weight Home Dec fabric
- Cut 2 main panels
- Cut 2 side panels

---

3 APPLY THE FUSIBLE INTERFACING AND FLEECE.

Note: See page 172 for interfacing application tips.

a. On the **Wrong** side of one fleece main panel, use your ruler and fabric marker and measure and mark ½" (1.3 cm) in around the entire edge. Draw a line connecting the marks and cut along the marked lines. Repeat to cut off the ½" (1.3 cm) seam allowance* around the remaining fleece main panel(s) and all fleece side panels.

b. Place the **Wrong** side of the first exterior main panel onto the fusible side of the coordinating interfacing piece. Using a damp pressing cloth,* fuse the interfacing in place, following the manufacturer's instructions. Turn the panel over and press it again, making sure there are no puckers.

c. Center the fusible side of the corresponding fleece panel onto the *interfaced* side of the first main panel. Fuse the fleece to the panel. Turn the panel over and press it again, making sure there are no puckers.

d. Repeat steps 3b and 3c to apply the corresponding interfacing and fleece pieces onto the second exterior main panel and both exterior side panels.

e. Repeat step 3b to fuse the corresponding interfacing pieces onto both yokes, lining side panels, lining main panels, and all 4 inside pocket panels (or just 2 if using mid-weight Home Dec fabric).

---

4 ATTACH THE YOKES TO THE EXTERIOR MAIN PANEL.

a. Using tracing paper and a tracing wheel or chalk pencil, transfer* the placement line for the yoke from the main panel pattern piece onto the **Right** side of each exterior main panel.

b. Stay stitch* ¼" (0.6 cm) from the outside curved edge on each yoke.

c. Place the first yoke with the *interfaced* side facing up. Fold the outside curved edge ¼" (0.6 cm) in along the stay stitching, and press.

d. Place the *interfaced* side of the yoke onto the **Right** side of the first main panel, lining up the folded edge on the yoke with the placement line on the main panel, and pin in place. Edge stitch* around the pinned edge and backstitch* at each end.

e. Sew a stay-stitching line $3/8$" (1 cm) from the top inside curved edge. This will hold the main panel and yoke in place and support the edges.

f. Clip into the seam allowance every $1/2$" to $3/4$" (1.3 cm to 1.9 cm) around the curve on the yoke. Be careful not to clip your stitching.

g. Repeat steps 4b through 4f to attach the second yoke to the second exterior main panel.

---

5 ATTACH THE TRIM TO THE MAIN PANELS.

a. Starting at the top outer edge of the first main panel, place the tape of the trim even with the outer curved edge and pin it in place. Ease and pin the trim around the edge, ending at the top edge on the other side. Cut off the excess trim.

Figure 1

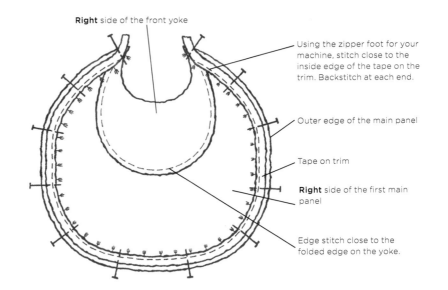

Right side of the front yoke

Using the zipper foot for your machine, stitch close to the inside edge of the tape on the trim. Backstitch at each end.

Outer edge of the main panel

Tape on trim

Right side of the first main panel

Edge stitch close to the folded edge on the yoke.

b. Using the zipper foot for your machine, stitch close to the inside edge of the tape along the pinned edge. Backstitch at each end.

c. Repeat steps 5a and 5b to attach the trim to the second main panel.

---

6 ATTACH THE EXTERIOR SIDE AND MAIN PANELS.

a. Place the two exterior side panels **Right** sides together, matching the raw edges. Pin along one short raw edge. Stitch a $1/2$" (1.3 cm) seam along the pinned edge. Backstitch at each end. Press the seam allowance open.

b. Topstitch* ¼" (0.6 cm) on each side of the seam that attaches the side panels together. Backstitch at each end. The seam will be the center bottom of the finished bag.

c. Fold the first main panel in half lengthwise, matching the side edges, and gently press a crease at the top and bottom of the folded edge to mark the center of the panel.

d. Place the bottom of the center crease on the first main panel on top of the seam on the side panel, **Right** sides together, and pin in place. Ease the curved edge on the main panel along the side panel, pinning as you go.

Figure 2

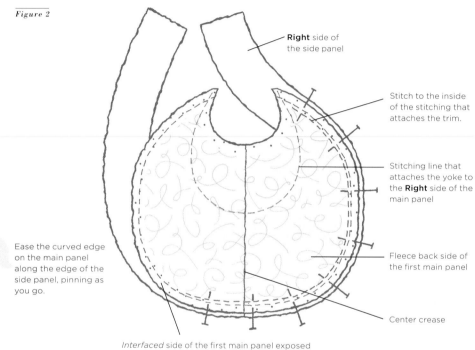

Right side of the side panel

Stitch to the inside of the stitching that attaches the trim.

Stitching line that attaches the yoke to the **Right** side of the main panel

Fleece back side of the first main panel

Center crease

Ease the curved edge on the main panel along the edge of the side panel, pinning as you go.

Interfaced side of the first main panel exposed around the edges

e. Stitch the panels together just to the inside of the stitching line that attached the trim to the main panel. Backstitch at each end.

f. Repeat steps 6c through 6e to attach the second main and side panels.

g. Attach the top short ends of each side panel to make the handle for the bag. Place the 2 short ends **Right** sides together and pin in place. Stitch a ½" (1.3 cm) seam across the pinned edge. Backstitch at each end. Press the seam allowance open. (See figure 3 on page 110.)

h. Topstitch ¼" (0.6 cm) on each side of the seam that attaches the side panels together. Backstitch at each end.

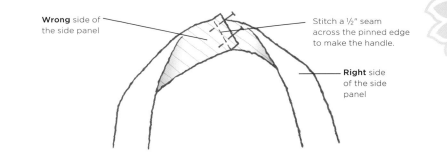

Wrong side of the side panel

Stitch a ½" seam across the pinned edge to make the handle.

Right side of the side panel

Figure 3

---

7   **MAKE AND ATTACH THE INSIDE POCKETS TO THE LINING MAIN PANELS.**

a. Place one *interfaced* inside pocket panel and one without **Right** sides together, matching the top inside curved edges. (Or, if using the light- to mid-weight fabric, place two interfaced inside pocket panels together.) Pin along the top edge. Stitch a ½" (1.3 cm) seam along the pinned edge. Backstitch at each end.

b. Clip V-shapes into the seam allowance every ½" to ¾" (1.3 cm to 1.9 cm) around the inside curved edge. Be careful not to clip the stitching.

c. Turn the inside pocket panel **Right** side out, matching the outer curved edges, and pin them together. Press along the inside finished edge.

d. Topstitch ½" (1.3 cm) from the inside finished edge. Backstitch at each end. Then, machine baste* a ¼" (0.6 cm) seam around the outer curved edges.

e. Place the inside pocket onto the **Right** side of one lining main panel, matching the outer curved edges. Pin and then machine baste in place.

f. Repeat steps 7a through 7e to make and attach the second inside pocket to the second lining main panel.

---

8   **ATTACH THE LINING MAIN PANELS AND SIDE PANEL.**

a. Repeat steps 6a through 6d to make the lining side panel and pin it to the lining main panel.

b. Stitch a ⅝" (1.6 cm) seam along the pinned edges to attach the lining main and side panels. Backstitch at each end. *Note: The larger seam allowance will allow the lining to fit better inside the bag.*

c. Repeat steps 6c and 6d and step 8b to attach the second lining main panel to the other long edge of the lining side panel.

d. Repeat steps 6g and 6h to attach the top short ends of the lining side panels.

9 ATTACH THE EXTERIOR TO THE LINING OF THE BAG.

a. With the exterior **Right** side out and the lining **Wrong** side out, slide the lining over the exterior, matching the side seams. Pin them together around one of the inside curved edges and the handle. Stitch a ½" (1.3 cm) seam along the pinned edge. Backstitch at each end.

Figure 4

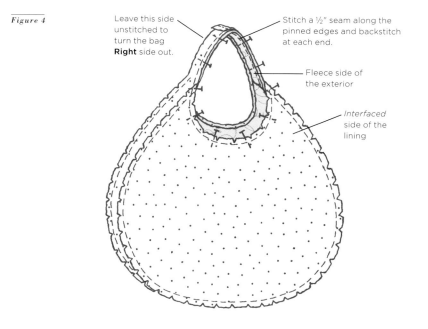

Leave this side unstitched to turn the bag **Right** side out.

Stitch a ½" seam along the pinned edges and backstitch at each end.

Fleece side of the exterior

Interfaced side of the lining

b. Turn the bag **Right** side out through the opening. Push the lining down inside the bag, pushing out all the edges. Press the bag.

c. Fold the other inside curved edge and long edge of the handle ½" (1.3 cm) in toward the *interfaced* side, and pin it in place. Repeat to fold ½" (1.3 cm) under on the exterior and lining of the bag. Pin the folded edges together.

d. Edge stitch along the pinned edge and backstitch at each end. Then, edge stitch along the finished edge around the other side handle opening. Backstitch at each end.

Your bag is complete! Take your Hobo Bag to the beach, to the market, or out on the town.

09

Blossom Handbag/ Shoulder Bag

Incredible lines and details make this semisoft bag a true showstopper. Handbag or shoulder bag—you choose!—it has both room and high fashion to spare. Multiple pockets on the interior of the large main compartment keep everything in place. (Only your sewing-savvy friends will believe you made it.)

Handbag

14" (35.6 cm) wide across the flap [15" (38.1 cm) wide across the bottom] x 8¹/₄" (21 cm) tall [13³/₄" (34.9 cm) tall with short handles] x 6" (15.2 cm) deep

Shoulder bag

14" (35.6 cm) wide across the flap [15" (38.1 cm) wide across the bottom] x 8¹/₄" (21 cm) tall [17³/₄" (45.1 cm) tall with long handles] x 6" (15.2 cm) deep

═══════════════════════════════════

FABRICS

• 1¹/₄ yd (1.14 m) of 54" (137 cm) wide mid-weight Home Dec print for the exterior
• ³/₄ yd (0.69 m) of 54" (137 cm) wide coordinating mid-weight Home Dec print for the lining
• ⁷/₈ yd (0.8 m) of 44" (112 cm) wide light- to mid-weight coordinating solid fabric for the divider panels

─ ─

**OTHER
SUPPLIES**

• 3 yd (2.74 m) of 20" (50.8 cm) wide fusible woven interfacing (I use Shape Flex SF-101 by Pellon)
• 2¹/₈ yd (1.94 m) of 20" (50.8 cm) wide Peltex #70 by Pellon or a similar extra-heavy stabilizer
• One 12" (30.5 cm) coordinating zipper (I use Coats brand)
• One size ³/₄" (1.9 cm) magnetic snap (I use Prym-Dritz brand)
• 1 spool coordinating all-purpose thread (I use Coats Dual Duty XP)

See Basic Tools Needed for Each Project (page 14).

─ ─

**ADDITIONAL
TOOLS
NEEDED**

• Masking tape
• Marker
• Hand sewing needle
• Safety pin
• Zipper foot for your sewing machine

Follow these instructions to make either size handle. Any measurement changes will be noted in the specific step.

1 CUT OUT THE PATTERN PIECES.

From the pattern sheet included with this book, cut out

• Main panel
• Divider panel
• Flap
• Handle bracket
• Side panel

2 CUT OUT ALL OF THE PIECES FROM THE FABRIC.

Tip: Using a piece of masking tape and a marker, write the name of each panel on the tape and place it on the individual fabric pieces to identify them.

a. Fold the fabrics in half lengthwise, **Wrong** sides together, matching the selvage edges,* and gently press a crease. Open the fabric and then fold the edges in 9" (23 cm) toward the **Wrong** side. This will give you enough folded edges to cut out all the pieces.

From the exterior fabric

• Cut 2 main panels on the fold*
• Cut 2 flaps on the fold
• Cut 2 side panels on the fold
• Cut 4 handle brackets

b. Open the fabric. Using a ruler and fabric marker, measure and mark the dimensions below directly onto the **Right** side of a single layer of fabric. Then, cut along the marked lines.
• Cut 1 bottom panel: 4$\frac{1}{2}$" (11.4 cm) wide x 16" (40.6 cm) long
• Cut 4 tags: 2" (5.1 cm) wide x 2$\frac{1}{2}$" (6.4 cm) long
• Cut 4 tie ends: 2" (5.1 cm) wide x 6$\frac{1}{2}$" (16.5 cm) long
• Cut 2 short handles for handbag: 4$\frac{1}{2}$" (11.4 cm) wide x 22" (55.9 cm) long
OR
• Cut 2 long handles for shoulder bag: 4$\frac{1}{2}$" (11.4 cm) wide x 30" (76.2 cm) long

From the lining fabric

• Cut 2 main panels on the fold
• Cut 2 side panels on the fold

c. Open the fabric. Measure and mark the dimensions for the bottom panel directly onto the **Right** side of a single layer of fabric. Then, cut along the marked lines.

• Cut 1 bottom panel: 4$\frac{1}{2}$" (11.4 cm) wide x 16" (40.6 cm) long

From the light- to mid-weight solid fabric

• Cut 8 divider panels on the fold

d. Use the panels you have cut out as full-size pattern pieces to cut the interfacing and Peltex.

From the fusible interfacing
• Cut 2 main panels
• Cut 2 flaps
• Cut 2 side panels
• Cut 4 divider panels
• Cut 4 handle brackets
• Cut 1 bottom panel
• Cut 4 tie ends
• Cut 2 handles

From the Peltex
• Cut 2 main panels
• Cut 1 flap
• Cut 2 side panels
• Cut 4 divider panels

e. On the Peltex main and side panels, the flap, and all 4 divider panels, using your ruler and marker, measure ½" (1.3 cm) in around the outside edges, and mark. Draw a line connecting the marks. Cut along the marked lines completely around each panel. This will reduce bulk in the seam allowances.

f. Measure and mark the dimensions below directly on the Peltex. Then, cut along the marked lines.
• Cut 1 bottom panel: 3½" (8.9 cm) wide x 15" (38.1 cm) long
• Cut 2 short handle inserts: 1⅛" (2.9 cm) wide x 21" (53.3 cm) long
OR
• Cut 2 long handle inserts: 1⅛" (2.9 cm) wide x 29" (73.7 cm) long

---

3 **APPLY THE FUSIBLE INTERFACINGS.**

Note: See page 172 for interfacing application tips.

a. On a flat surface, center the Peltex main panel on the **Wrong** side of the first exterior main panel, leaving ½" (1.3 cm) of the fabric showing around the outside edges.

b. Place the fusible side of the interfacing main panel onto the Peltex. Using a damp pressing cloth,* fuse it in place, sealing the edges and securing the Peltex. Turn the panel over and press it again, making sure there are no puckers.

c. Repeat steps 3a and 3b to attach the Peltex and interfacing to the second main panel, both exterior side panels, the bottom panel, 4 divider panels, and one of the flaps.

d. Place the fusible side of the second flap interfacing onto the **Wrong** side of the second flap. Match the edges and fuse it in place. This will be the lining flap.

e. Repeat step 3d to fuse the coordinating interfacing pieces to both handles, all 4 handle brackets, and the tie ends.

4 INSTALL THE MAGNETIC SNAP.

a. Fold the lining flap in half, **Right** sides together, matching the side edges. Gently press a crease along the folded edge. Open the flap.

b. Measure 1½" (3.8 cm) up on the crease from the center rounded edge and make a mark.

c. Center the male half of the magnetic snap over the crease and above the 1½" (3.8 cm) mark. Install the snap, following the manufacturer's instructions.

d. Repeat step 4a to mark the center of the front exterior main panel.

e. On the **Right** side of the exterior main panel, measure and mark 3½" (8.9 cm) down from the top edge on the center crease.

f. Center the female half of the snap over the crease and below the 3½" (8.9 cm) mark. Install the snap.

5 MAKE AND ATTACH THE HANDLE BRACKETS TO THE EXTERIOR MAIN PANELS.

a. Fold both long side edges of the first handle bracket ½" (1.3 cm) in toward the **Wrong** side, and press.

b. Topstitch* ⅜" (1 cm) from each folded edge and backstitch* at each end.

c. Fold the top edge 1" (2.5 cm) toward the **Wrong** side and pin it in place.

d. Place the bracket onto the **Right** side of the front exterior main panel, matching the bottom edges. Place the outside edge of the bracket 1¼" (3.2 cm) from the right edge of the main panel and pin it in place.

Figure 1

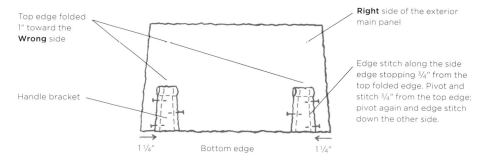

Top edge folded 1" toward the **Wrong** side

Handle bracket

Right side of the exterior main panel

Edge stitch along the side edge stopping ¾" from the top folded edge. Pivot and stitch ¾" from the top edge; pivot again and edge stitch down the other side.

1¼"   Bottom edge   1¼"

e. Starting at the bottom of the bracket, edge stitch* up along the side edge, stopping ¾" (1.9 cm) from the top edge. Pivot* and stitch ¾" (1.9 cm) from the top folded edge; pivot again and edge stitch down the other side edge. Backstitch at each end.

f. Repeat steps 5a through 5e to make and attach a second bracket to the left bottom corner on the front main panel. Then, attach the last 2 brackets to both bottom corners on the back main panel.

6   MAKE THE HANDLES.

a. Fold the first handle in half lengthwise, **Wrong** sides together, and press a crease along the folded edge.

b. Open the handle. Fold each long edge in to meet the center crease, and press.

c. Tuck the Peltex handle insert under one of the folded edges, leaving $\frac{1}{2}$" (1.3 cm) of the handle showing on each end of the Peltex.

d. Fold the handle in half again at the center crease, enclosing the raw edges. Press and pin.

e. Edge stitch down both folded edges and backstitch at each end.

f. Repeat steps 6a through 6e to make the second handle.

7   MAKE THE TIE ENDS.

Repeat steps 6a, 6b, 6d, and 6e to make all 4 tie ends.

8   INSERT THE TIE ENDS INTO THE BRACKETS.

a. Attach a safety pin to one end of the first tie.

b. Pull the tie through one bracket, centering it within the bracket. Remove the safety pin.

c. Repeat steps 8a and 8b to insert the next three tie ends into the other three brackets.

9   ATTACH THE HANDLES AND TIE ENDS TO THE MAIN PANELS.

a. Match the ends of the first tie and place them onto the end of one handle, overlapping by $\frac{1}{2}$" (1.3 cm). Be careful not to twist the tie. Pin the ends in place. Stitch across the ends of the handle and the tie. Backstitch at each end. (See Figure 2.)

b. Trim the raw ends of the tie to $\frac{1}{8}$" (0.3 cm).

c. Place this end of the handle onto the main panel, centering the handle $1\frac{1}{4}$" (3.2 cm) up from the folded end of the handle bracket. Pin in place. Using a tight, wide zigzag stitch, satin stitch across the end of the tie end to secure it in place and conceal the raw edges. Backstitch at each end.

d. Repeat steps 9a through 9c to attach the other end of the handle to the tie on the opposite side of the same main panel. Be careful not to twist the handle.

e. Repeat steps 9a through 9d to attach the second handle to the remaining ties on the other main panel.

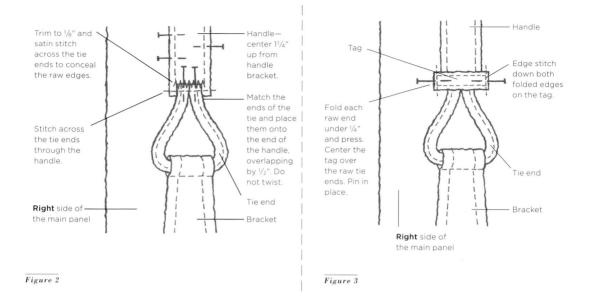

Figure 2

Trim to ⅛" and satin stitch across the tie ends to conceal the raw edges.

Stitch across the tie ends through the handle.

Right side of the main panel

Handle—center 1¼" up from handle bracket.

Match the ends of the tie and place them onto the end of the handle, overlapping by ½". Do not twist.

Tie end

Bracket

Figure 3

Tag

Fold each raw end under ¼" and press. Center the tag over the raw tie ends. Pin in place.

Right side of the main panel

Handle

Edge stitch down both folded edges on the tag.

Tie end

Bracket

10 MAKE AND ATTACH THE TAGS.

a. Repeat steps 6a, 6b, 6d, and 6e to make all 4 tags to cover the stitching that attaches the tie to the handle.

b. Fold the first tag under ¼" (0.6 cm) on each raw end and press in place.

c. Center the tag over the stitching that attached the handle and ties together, and pin in place. (See Figure 3.)

d. Edge stitch down both folded edges to attach the tag. Backstitch at each end.

e. Repeat steps 10b through 10d to attach the other 3 tags to cover the stitching that attaches the ties to the handles.

11 MAKE THE EXTERIOR.

a. Place the bottom edge of the front main panel and one long edge of the bottom panel **Right** sides together and pin in place. Stitch a ½" (1.3 cm) seam across the pinned edge. Backstitch at each end. Press the seam allowances* toward the bottom panel.

b. Repeat step 11a to attach the back main panel to the other long edge of the bottom panel.

c. Place the side edges of the first side panel **Right** sides together with the main and bottom panels, matching the top edges. Pin the panels together, easing the main panel around the curved edge of the side panel. Stitch a ½" (1.3 cm) seam down the pinned edges, starting and stopping at the top edges on the main panels. Backstitch at each end.

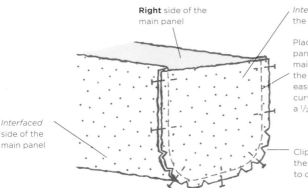

Right side of the main panel

Interfaced side of the side panel

Place the side edges of the first side panel **Right** sides together with the main and bottom panels matching the edges. Pin the panels together, easing the main panel around the curved edge of the side panel. Stitch a ½" seam down the pinned edge.

Interfaced side of the main panel

Clip in the seam allowance along the curved edge, being careful not to clip the stitching.

Figure 4

d. Repeat step 11c to attach the second side panel to the other side edges on the main and bottom panels.

e. Clip* in the seam allowance along the curved edge, being careful not to clip your stitching.

Please set the exterior aside.

MAKE THE FLAP.

a. Place the exterior and lining flaps **Right** sides together, matching the edges, and pin them in place.

b. Stitch a ½" (1.3 cm) seam around the pinned edges, leaving an 8" (20.3 cm) opening centered on the long straight edge of the flap. Backstitch at each end.

c. Trim* the corners in the seam allowance making sure not to clip the stitching. Then, trim the seam allowance to ¼" (0.6 cm) along the rounded corners and across the front rounded edge.

d. Clip in the seam allowance around the curved edges every ½" to ¾" (1.3 cm to 1.9 cm) to allow the flap to lay flat when turned **Right** side out.

e. Turn the flap **Right** side out, using a turning tool* to gently push out the corners, and press.

f. Fold each side of the opening under ½" (1.3 cm) toward the **Wrong** side, and press. Pin the edges together. Edge stitch ⅛" (0.3 cm) from the finished edge completely around the flap. This will close the opening and secure the Peltex inside.

Please set the flap aside.

13 MAKE THE LINING FOR THE BAG.

Repeat steps 11a through 11e to make the lining for the bag.

14 ATTACH THE LINING TO THE EXTERIOR.

a. With the exterior **Right** side out and the lining **Wrong** side out, slip the lining over the exterior, matching the top edges and side seams. Tuck the handles down between the two layers and pin in place.

b. Stitch a ½" (1.3 cm) seam around the top edge, leaving a 10" (25.4 cm) opening centered along the back main panel. Backstitch at each end.

c. Turn the bag **Right** side out through the opening along the back main panel. Push the lining down inside. Gently push out the seams and press along the top edge.

d. Fold each side of the opening under ½" (1.3 cm) toward the **Wrong** side, and press. Pin it together. Edge stitch completely around the top edge and backstitch at each end.

15 ATTACH THE FLAP TO THE BACK OF THE BAG.

a. Using your ruler and fabric marker, measure and mark 1½" (3.8 cm) in from each side edge along the long straight edge on the exterior flap.

b. Measure and mark ¾" (1.9 cm) down from the top edge on each end of the back of the bag. Line up the two marks and draw a line connecting them.

c. Center the long straight edge of the flap along the marked line on the back of the bag and pin it in place.

d. Starting at the first 1½" (3.8 cm) mark on the flap, edge stitch over the existing stitching, stopping at the mark on the opposite side. Backstitch at each end.

e. Topstitch ⅜" (1 cm) from the first stitching line, starting and stopping at the 1½" (3.8 cm) marks. Then, again topstitch ⅜" (1 cm) from the second stitching line, making sure to catch the top edge of the bag underneath. Backstitch at each end.

Please set the bag aside.

16 MAKE THE DIVIDERS.

a. Place one *interfaced* divider panel and one without interfacing **Right** sides together, matching all the edges. Pin in place.

b. Stitch a ½" (1.3 cm) seam around the panels, leaving a 10" (25.4 cm) opening centered along the bottom edge. Backstitch at each end.

c. Trim all the corners in the seam allowance, making sure not to clip your stitching.

d. Turn the divider panel **Right** side out through the opening. Use a turning tool to gently push out the corners. Press the panel flat. Fold each edge of the opening under ½" (1.3 cm) toward the **Wrong** side, and press. Pin the opening closed. *Note: You will stitch the opening closed in step 16g.*

e. Repeat steps 16a through 16d to make a second divider panel.

f. Place both divider panels together. Match and then pin around all the edges.

g. Edge stitch close to the finished edges, down both sides and across the bottom edges. Backstitch at each end. You have completed the first divider. Set this divider aside while you make one with a zipper closure.

h. On the third *interfaced* divider panel, place the zipper and panel **Right** sides together, with the edge of the zipper tape ¼" (0.6 cm) down from the top edge of the panel. Align the head of the zipper ½" (1.3 cm) from the side edge and pin it in place. Fold the end of the tape so it angles off the top edge of the divider panel on each end of the zipper.

i. Using the zipper foot for your machine, stitch ⅛" (0.3 cm) from the coils. Backstitch at each end.

j. Place this divider panel and one without interfacing **Right** sides together, matching the edges, and pin. *Note: The zipper is sandwiched between the panels.* On the *interfaced* side of the divider panel, stitch a ½" (1.3 cm) seam around the panels leaving a 10" (25.4 cm) opening centered along the bottom edge. Backstitch at each end.

k. Trim the corners in the seam allowance, making sure not to clip your stitching.

l. Turn the divider panel **Right** side out, pulling out the zipper through the opening. Use a turning tool to gently push out the corners. Press the panel flat. Fold each edge of the opening under ½" (1.3 cm) toward the **Wrong** side, and press. Pin the opening closed. *Note: You will stitch the opening closed in step 16o.*

m. Repeat steps 16h through 16l to make and attach the last two divider panels onto the other long edge of the zipper.

n. Place both divider panels together, with the **Right** side of the zipper on the top outside edge. Pin down the sides and across the bottom edges of the divider.

o. Edge stitch close to the finished edges down the sides and across the bottom edges. Backstitch at each end.

17 ATTACH THE DIVIDERS TO THE INSIDE OF THE BAG.

a. Working on one of the exterior side panels, measure 1¾" (4.4 cm) in from both the front and back seams across the top finished edge of the side panel, and mark. Repeat to mark the same measurements on the second side panel. You will attach the divider without the zipper between the front set of marks and the zippered divider between the back set.

Figure 5

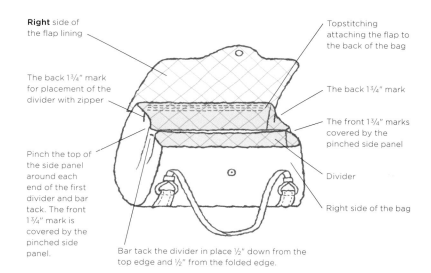

Right side of the flap lining

Topstitching attaching the flap to the back of the bag

The back 1¾" mark for placement of the divider with zipper

The back 1¾" mark

The front 1¾" marks covered by the pinched side panel

Pinch the top of the side panel around each end of the first divider and bar tack. The front 1¾" mark is covered by the pinched side panel.

Divider

Right side of the bag

Bar tack the divider in place ½" down from the top edge and ½" from the folded edge.

b. Place the divider without a zipper inside the bag. Line up each end of the divider with the two front marks. Then, pinch the top of the side panel around each end of the divider and pin through all the layers.

c. Bar tack* the divider in place, ½" (1.3 cm) down from the top edge and ½" (1.3 cm) in from the folded edge. If the fabric layers are too thick for your machine, bar tack by hand with a double strand of thread, stitching a few times in place. Tie off securely.

d. Repeat steps 17b and 17c to attach the zippered divider between the back set of marks.

Your Blossom Bag is complete! Show your new custom designer handbag to the world—you can bet nobody else has one just like it.

10 Everything Wristlet

Named "Everything" as in "everything you need," this is the ultimate mini carryall with elegant lines. In two sizes (the large one acts as a great on-the-go bag), with a strong interfacing to give it wonderful body and shape as well as a pretty wrist strap, this charming bag has it all. Pleated sides and interior pockets make for easy access.

FINISHED SIZES	**Small wristlet** 8" (20.3 cm) wide x 5" (12.7 cm) tall x 1³/₄" (4.4 cm) deep **Large wristlet** 10" (25.4 cm) wide x 7" (17.9 cm) tall x 1³/₄" (4.4 cm) deep

==

FABRICS

From 44" (112 cm) wide light- to mid-weight fabric

For small wristlet:
• ¹/₄ yd (0.23 m) of one print for the exterior flap
• ³/₈ yd (0.34 m) of a coordinating solid for the exterior and handle
• ⁵/₈ yd (0.57 m) of a coordinating print for the lining

For large wristlet:
• ¹/₄ yd (0.23 m) of one print for the exterior flap
• ¹/₂ yd (0.46 m) of a coordinating solid for the exterior and handle
• ⁷/₈ yd (0.8 m) of a coordinating print for the lining

OTHER SUPPLIES

• 1¹/₄ yd (1.14 m) of 20" (50.8 cm) wide fusible woven interfacing (I use Shape Flex SF-101 by Pellon)
• ¹/₂ yd (0.46 m) of 20" (50.8 cm) wide Peltex #70 by Pellon or a similar extra-heavy stabilizer
• One ¹/₂" (1.3 cm) magnetic snap (I use Prym-Dritz brand)
• 1 spool coordinating all-purpose thread (I use Coats Dual Duty XP)
• One 7" (17.9 cm) coordinating zipper for the small wristlet (I use Coats brand)
OR
• One 12" (30.5 cm) coordinating zipper for the large wristlet

See Basic Tools Needed for Each Project (page 14).

ADDITIONAL TOOLS NEEDED

• Masking tape
• Marker
• Hand sewing needle
• Zipper foot for your sewing machine

Follow these instructions for making either size wristlet. Any measurement changes will be noted in the specific steps.

---

1 CUT OUT THE FLAP PATTERN PIECE FROM THE PATTERN SHEET INCLUDED WITH THIS BOOK.

---

2 CUT OUT ALL OF THE PIECES FROM THE FABRIC.

Tip: Using a piece of masking tape and a marker, write the name of each panel on the tape and place it on the individual fabric pieces to identify them.

a. Fold the exterior print in half lengthwise, **Wrong** sides together, matching the selvage edges*. Gently press a crease on the fold. Open the fabric and fold the selvage edge in to meet the center crease. This will give you enough folded edges to cut out the flaps.

From the exterior print fabric
• Cut 2 flaps on the fold*

b. Using ruler and fabric marker, measure and mark the dimensions below directly on the **Right** side of a single layer of fabric. Then, cut along the marked lines.

From the solid exterior fabric
For small wristlet:
• Cut 1 main panel: 11" (27.9 cm) wide x 12" (30.5 cm) long
• Cut 1 handle: 2" (5.1 cm) wide x 10³/₄" (27.3 cm) long

For large wristlet:
• Cut 1 main panel: 13" (33 cm) wide x 15" (38.1 cm) long
• Cut 1 handle: 2" (5.1 cm) wide x 10³/₄" (27.3 cm) long

From the lining fabric
For small wristlet:
• Cut 1 lining panel: 10¹/₂" (26.7 cm) wide x 18¹/₂" (47 cm) long
• Cut 2 card pocket panels: 6³/₄" (17.1 cm) wide x 16" (40.6 cm) long
• Cut 2 zipper end pieces: 4" (10.2 cm) wide x 1¹/₂" (3.8 cm) long

For large wristlet:
• Cut 1 lining panel: 12¹/₂" (31.8 cm) wide x 21¹/₂" (54.6 cm) long
• Cut 2 card pocket panels: 8³/₄" (22.2 cm) wide x 24¹/₂" (62.2 cm) long
• Cut 2 zipper end pieces: 4" (10.2 cm) wide x 1¹/₂" (3.8 cm) long

c. Open the fabric flap and use it as a full-size pattern piece to cut out the interfacing and Peltex pieces.

From the fusible interfacing

For small wristlet:
- Cut 2 flaps
- Cut 1 main panel: 11" (27.9 cm) wide x 12" (30.5 cm) long
- Cut 1 lining panel: 10½" (26.7 cm) wide x 18½" (47 cm) long
- Cut 2 card pocket panels: 6¾" (17.1 cm) wide x 16" (40.6 cm) long
- Cut 1 handle: 2" (5 cm) wide x 10¾" (27.3 cm) long

For large wristlet:
- Cut 2 flaps
- Cut 1 main panel: 13" (33 cm) wide x 15" (38.1 cm) long
- Cut 1 lining panel: 12½" (31.8 cm) wide x 21½" (54.6 cm) long
- Cut 2 card pocket panels: 8¾" (22.2 cm) wide x 24½" (62.2 cm) long
- Cut 1 handle: 2" (5 cm) wide x 10¾" (27.3 cm) long

From the Peltex

For small wristlet:
- Cut 1 flap and then trim ½" (1.3 cm) off each side edge and 1" (2.5 cm) off the top straight edge
- Cut 2 front/back pieces: 8" (20.3 cm) wide x 4½" (11.4 cm) long
- Cut 2 card pocket pieces: 6¼" (15.9 cm) wide x 4" (10.2 cm) long
- Cut 1 bottom panel: 8" (20.3 cm) wide x 1½" (3.8 cm) long

For large wristlet:
- Cut 1 flap and then trim ½" (1.3 cm) off each side edge and 1" (2.5 cm) off the top straight edge
- Cut 2 front/back pieces: 10" (25.4 cm) wide x 6" (15.2 cm) long
- Cut 2 card pocket pieces: 8¼" (21 cm) wide x 5½" (14 cm) long
- Cut 1 bottom panel: 10" (25.4 cm) wide x 1½" (3.8 cm) long

3

APPLY THE FUSIBLE INTERFACINGS.

Note: See page 172 for interfacing application tips.

a. On a flat surface, place the first Peltex front/back piece onto the **Wrong** side of the exterior main panel ½" (1.3 cm) down from the top 11" (27.9 cm) edge (for small bag) or 13" (33 cm) edge (for large bag) and 1½" (3.8 cm) in from each side edge. Place the second front/back piece along the bottom edge of the main panel using the same measurements. There will be a 2" (5.1 cm) space between the two Peltex pieces at the center of the main panel. Then, center the Peltex bottom panel between the 2 front/back pieces.

b. Place the fusible side of the interfacing main panel onto the Peltex, making sure it doesn't move. Using a damp pressing cloth,* fuse in place, sealing the edges around the Peltex. Turn the panel over and press it again, making sure there are no puckers. Set aside.

c. Place the **Wrong** side of the lining panel onto the fusible side of the corresponding interfacing. Fuse them together. Repeat to fuse the interfacing to the exterior and lining flaps and handle.

d. On the **Right** side of the first card pocket panel, using your ruler and chalk pencil, measure 4½" (11.4 cm) (for small bag) or 5½" (14 cm) (for large bag) down from the top edge along each side edge, and mark. Then, draw a line to connect the marks.

e. Fold the panel, **Wrong** sides together, along the marked line. Gently press a crease along the folded edge, then open the panel.

f. Place the card pocket panel **Wrong** side up. Center the corresponding Peltex piece ½" (1.3 cm) down from one short edge, leaving ¼" (0.6 cm) of fabric exposed on each side.

g. Place the fusible side of the corresponding interfacing onto the Peltex and the **Wrong** side of the card pocket panel, making sure not to move the Peltex. Fuse it in place, sealing the edges around the Peltex. Turn the panel over and press it again, making sure there are no puckers.

h. Repeat steps 3d through 3g to fuse the second Peltex piece to the second card pocket panel.

4 **MAKE THE EXTERIOR.**

a. On the **Right** side of the exterior main panel, mark the placement for the magnetic snap. Measure 5½" (14 cm) (for small bag) or 6½" (16.5 cm) (for large bag) across the top edge of the main panel and place a pin to mark the center of the panel. Then, measure 2½" (6.4 cm) (for small bag) or 4½" (11.4 cm) (for large bag) down from the center and make a mark.

b. Center the female half of the magnetic snap below the 2½" (6.4 cm) (for small bag) or 4½" (11.4 cm) (for large bag) mark and install the snap following the manufacturer's instructions.

c. *Note: The Peltex pieces are sandwiched between the main panel and the interfacing with a ¼" (0.6 cm) space between each Peltex piece.* Fold the main panel with the *interfaced* sides together, matching the bottom edges of the first Peltex front/back piece and the edge of the Peltex bottom panel. Edge stitch* across the folded edge, catching only the fabric between the two panels. Backstitch* at each end. Repeat to edge stitch along the bottom edge of the other Peltex piece.

d. Fold the main panel in half, **Right** sides together, matching the top and bottom 11" (27.9 cm) (for small bag) or 13" (33 cm) (for large bag) edges. Pin down each of the short side edges that form. Stitch a ½" (1.3 cm) seam down the pinned edges and backstitch at each end.

e. Make a 2" (5.1 cm) gusset* at one of the bottom corners of the main panel by matching the side seam with the center of the bottom panel, forming a triangle in the corner. Measure 1" (2.5 cm) in from the point along the side seam and make a mark. Draw a straight line across the corner at the mark.

f. Stitch along the marked line, creating a gusset. Backstitch at each end. Trim the corner to create a ½" (1.3 cm) seam allowance*.

g. Repeat steps 4e and 4f to make the gusset on the other bottom corner of the main panel.

h. Turn the exterior **Right** side out, using a turning tool* to gently push out the corners. Press all the seams.

Please set the exterior aside.

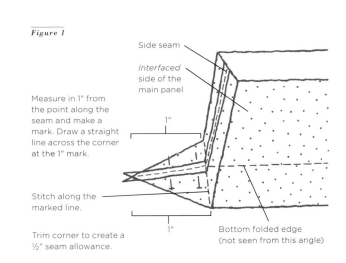

Figure 1

Side seam

Interfaced side of the main panel

Measure in 1" from the point along the seam and make a mark. Draw a straight line across the corner at the 1" mark.

1"

Stitch along the marked line.

Trim corner to create a ½" seam allowance.

1"

Bottom folded edge (not seen from this angle)

---

5 MAKE THE FLAP.

a. Fold the lining flap in half, **Right** sides together, matching the side edges. Gently press a crease along the folded edge. Open the flap.

b. On the **Right** side of the flap, measure and mark 1" (2.5 cm) up from the rounded edge on the center.

c. Center the male half of the magnetic snap above the mark, and install the snap.

d. Place the exterior and lining flaps **Right** sides together, matching the edges, and pin them in place. Stitch a ½" (1.3 cm) seam down both sides and across the bottom. Backstitch at each end.

e. Use your scissors to trim* the corners and clip* V-shapes in the seam allowances every ½" (1.3 cm) around the curve, making sure not to clip your stitching.

f. Turn the flap **Right** side out. Use a turning tool to gently push out the corners. Press the flap flat.

g. Insert the Peltex flap between the panels through the unstitched top. Place the seam allowances on top of the Peltex on the lining side of the flap. Push it snug up against the seams. Pin it in place.

h. Machine baste* a ¼" (0.6 cm) seam across the top edges, enclosing the Peltex.

i. Topstitch* ⅛" (0.3 cm) from the side and curved bottom edges, securing the Peltex. Backstitch at each end.

6 MAKE AND ATTACH THE HANDLE TO THE FLAP.

a. Fold the handle in half lengthwise, *interfaced* sides together, and press a crease along the folded edge. Open the handle.

b. Fold each long edge in to meet the center crease, and press.

c. Fold the handle in half again at the center crease to enclose the raw edges, and press. Pin along the folded edge.

d. Edge stitch down each long edge and backstitch at each end.

e. Fold the handle in half, matching the short ends. Pin the ends together.

f. On the exterior flap, place the end of the handle ½" (1.3 cm) in from the left side along the top raw edge. Match the edges, pin, and then machine baste them in place.

7 ATTACH THE FLAP TO THE MAIN PANEL.

a. Center the exterior flap onto the **Right** side of the back main panel, matching the raw edges. Pin together.

b. Stitch a ½" (1.3 cm) seam along the pinned edge. Backstitch at each end. Press the seam allowances toward the main panel.

Please set the exterior of the bag aside.

8 MAKE THE CENTER POCKET.

Note: You will make two card pockets and then attach them to make the center pocket.

a. Fold the first card pocket panel along the crease you made in step 3e with *interfaced* sides together matching the side edges. Place the longer 11½" (29.2 cm) (for small bag) or 13½" (34.3 cm) (for large bag) side of the panel **Right** side up.

Figure 2

This illustration shows the pressed edges before pinning the edges together in step 8e.

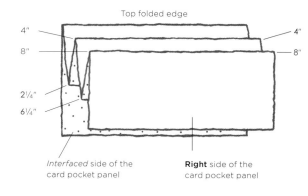

Top folded edge

4"
8"

4"
8"

2¼"
6¼"

Interfaced side of the card pocket panel

Right side of the card pocket panel

b. Starting at the first folded edge and using your ruler and chalk pencil, measure and mark down each side edge following these measurements:

For small bag: $2\frac{1}{4}$" (5.7 cm), 4" (10.2 cm), $6\frac{1}{4}$" (15.9 cm), and 8" (20.3 cm). Continue with these additional measurements to make 2 more pockets.

For large bag: $10\frac{1}{4}$" (26 cm), 12" (30.5 cm), $14\frac{1}{4}$" (36.2 cm), and 16" (40.6 cm) Line up each set of marks and draw a line between them.

c. Fold the pocket panel, **Right** sides together, along the $2\frac{1}{4}$" (5.7 cm) line and press along the folded edge.

d. Fold the panel back at the 4" (10.2 cm) line, with *interfaced* sides together. Press along the folded edge.

e. Continue this process, folding the panel, **Right** sides together, along the $6\frac{1}{4}$" (15.9 cm) line and then back with the *interfaced* sides together along the 8" (20.3 cm) line. Continue to fold across the other measurements to make 2 additional pockets for the large bag. Press and pin the panel along each edge.

f. Fold each bottom edge $\frac{1}{2}$" (1.3 cm) in toward the *interfaced* side, and press. Match the folded edges and pin them together. Machine baste a $\frac{1}{4}$" (0.6 cm) seam down both sides to hold the folded compartments in place. You will stitch the bottom edges together once the other side of the card pocket is completed. This makes one side of the center pocket.

For the large bag only, fold the card pocket panel in half, matching the short sides. Place a pin at the top and bottom of the fold to mark the center of the panel. Draw a line connecting the pins. Starting at the bottom of the pocket, stitch up, following the line to make more compartments for your cards. Backstitch at each end.

g. Repeat steps 8a through 8f to make the other side of the center pocket.

h. Place each panel with the pocket compartments facing out. Match the side and bottom edges and pin them together.

i. Edge stitch across the pinned bottom edges and backstitch at each end.

j. Machine baste a $\frac{1}{4}$" (0.6 cm) seam down each side edge to hold the panels together.

Please set the center pocket aside.

- -

9 INSTALL THE ZIPPER ON THE LINING PANEL.

a. On a flat surface, place the lining panel with the **Right** side up. Using your ruler and chalk pencil, measure and mark the following dimensions from the top, down each side edge: $1\frac{1}{8}$" (2.9 cm), $4\frac{5}{8}$" (11.7 cm), and $8\frac{1}{8}$" (20.6 cm). Line up each set of marks and draw a line between them.

b. Measure 2" (5.1 cm) in from each side along the $1\frac{1}{8}$" (2.9 cm) chalk line and mark.

c. Fold each zipper end piece in half, **Wrong** sides together, matching the $1\frac{1}{2}$" (3.8 cm) edges, and press along the folded edge.

d. Place the first folded edge of the zipper end piece at the 2" (5.1 cm) mark, with ⅜" (1 cm) of the end piece edge hanging below the chalk line. Pin in place. Repeat to attach the second end piece on the right edge.

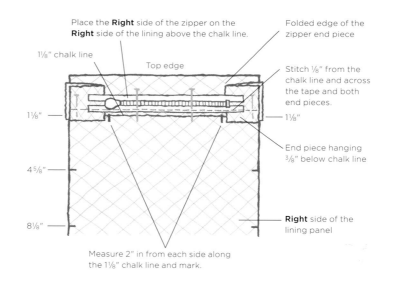

Figure 3

Place the **Right** side of the zipper on the **Right** side of the lining above the chalk line.

Folded edge of the zipper end piece

1⅛" chalk line

Top edge

Stitch ⅛" from the chalk line and across the tape and both end pieces.

1⅛"

1⅛"

End piece hanging ⅜" below chalk line

4⅝"

8⅛"

Right side of the lining panel

Measure 2" in from each side along the 1⅛" chalk line and mark.

e. Place the closed zipper and lining panel **Right** sides together. Align the top of the zipper head even with the left 2" (5.1 cm) mark and the long edge of the zipper tape just above the chalk line. Pin in place.

f. Using the zipper foot for your machine, stitch ⅛" (0.3 cm) from the coils on the tape, starting and stopping at the side edges of the end pieces. Backstitch at each end.

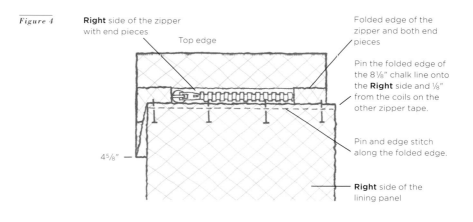

Figure 4

Right side of the zipper with end pieces

Top edge

Folded edge of the zipper and both end pieces

Pin the folded edge of the 8⅛" chalk line onto the **Right** side and ⅛" from the coils on the other zipper tape.

4⅝"

Pin and edge stitch along the folded edge.

Right side of the lining panel

g. Fold the zipper and both end pieces over at the stitching, so the **Right** side is facing up. Press along the folded edge. Edge stitch along the folded edge of the end pieces and the zipper tape. Backstitch at each end. (See Figure 4 on page 137.)

h. Fold the panel **Right** sides together, across the $4^5/_8"$ (11.7 cm) chalk line, and press along the folded edge. Then, fold the panel back toward the *interfaced* side across the $8^1/_8"$ (20.6 cm) chalk line, and press.

i. Pin the folded edge of the $8^1/_8"$ (20.6 cm) chalk line onto the **Right** side and $^1/_8"$ (0.3 cm) from the coils on the other side of the zipper tape. Continue to pin the folded edge across each end piece.

j. Open the zipper. Then, edge stitch along the pinned edge and backstitch at each end. Close the zipper. *Note: Do not stitch through the back of the pocket.*

---

10 MAKE THE LINING AND GUSSETS.

a. Fold the lining panel in half **Right** sides together, matching the $10^1/_2"$ (26.7 cm) (for small bag) or $12^1/_2"$ (31.8 cm) (for large bag) edges. Place the center pocket in between the lining panel, matching the left side edges. *Note: The center pocket is not as wide or as long as the lining panel, which will form the sides and bottom of the Wristlet.*

b. Place the top edge of the center pocket $^5/_8"$ (1.6 cm) down from the top edge of the lining panel and pin down the left side edge. Stitch a $^1/_4"$ (0.6 cm) seam down the pinned edge. Backstitch at each end.

c. Next, make the gusset. Move the center pocket to one side out of your way. Match the side seam to the bottom center crease, forming a triangle in the corner. Measure 1" (2.5 cm) in from the point along the seam and make a mark. Draw a straight line across the corner at the 1" (2.5 cm) mark. Pin them together. (See Figure 1 on page 134.)

d. Stitch along the marked line, creating a gusset. Backstitch at each end. Trim the corner to create a $^1/_2"$ (1.3 cm) seam allowance.

e. Pull the right side edge of the center pocket over and place it $^5/_8"$ (1.6 cm) down from the top edge on the **Right** side of the lining panel. Pin in place. Stitch a $^1/_4"$ (0.6 cm) seam down the pinned edge. Backstitch at each end.

f. Repeat steps 10c and 10d to make the gusset on the other corner of the lining panel.

11 ATTACH THE EXTERIOR AND LINING PANELS.

a. Fold the top edges of the exterior panel ½" (1.3 cm) toward the **Wrong** side, and press. Then, fold the top edge of the lining panel ⅝" (1.6 cm) toward the **Wrong** side, and press.

b. With the **Right** side of the exterior facing out and the **Wrong** side of the lining out, slip the lining *inside* the exterior, placing the zippered lining pocket to the back of the bag (the side with the flap). Match the top folded edges and pin them together.

c. **Note: The exterior of the bag is facing out; stitch on the lining side, laying the center pocket flat and out of your way as you stitch up to it on each side of the bag. Be patient and go slowly, and you will get great results.** Starting on the front side of the center pocket on one side of the bag, edge stitch ⅛" (0.3 cm) from the top edge across the side and around the front, stopping at the front of the other side of the pocket. Backstitch at each end.

d. Starting again at the back of the pocket, edge stitch ⅛" (0.3 cm) from the top edge across the side and along the stitching that attaches the flap and stop at the back of the other side of the pocket. Backstitch at each end. Fold in the side edges and press the bag flat. **Note: If you have difficulty stitching up to the center pocket, stitch as close as you can and then hand stitch the remaining edges together.**

Your Everything Wristlet is complete! Everyone will wonder, "Is it a bag or a wallet?" Grin and tell them, "But, of course!"

11

Miss Maven Ruffled Handbag

With sassy handles and pretty ruffle trim, this bag is an absolute knockout. Its attributes include a faux bottom for a little extra support in just the right place. The small bag makes a charming notions keeper or a roomy purse for a romantic evening out; use the large bag for the gym, beach, or weekend travel. The Miss Maven will put style back into your routine.

FINISHED SIZES	**Small bag**
	18" (45.7 cm) wide at the bottom x 15½" (39.4 cm) tall x 3½" (8.9 cm) deep
	Large bag
	21½" (54.6 cm) wide at the bottom x 17¼" (43.8 cm) tall x 3½" (8.9 cm) deep

==

FABRICS	**From 44" (112 cm) wide light- to mid-weight fabric**
	For small bag:
	• 1 yd (0.91 m) of one print for the exterior main panels
	• 1 yd (0.91 m) of a coordinating solid for the exterior handles and ruffles
	• 1⅝ yd (1.49 m) of a coordinating print for the lining
	For large bag:
	• 1⅛ yd (1.03 m) of one print for the exterior main panels
	• 1 yd (0.91 m) of a coordinating solid for the exterior handles and ruffles
	• 1⅝ yd (1.49 m) of a coordinating print for the lining

- -

OTHER SUPPLIES	• 2⅞ yd (2.63 m) of 20" (50.8 cm) wide fusible woven interfacing (I use Shape Flex SF-101 by Pellon)
	• 1 yd (0.91 m) of 44" (112 cm) wide fusible fleece (I use fusible Thermolam Plus by Pellon)
	• ⅝ yd (0.57 m) of 20" (50.8 cm) wide double-sided fusible Peltex by Pellon or a similar extra-heavy stabilizer
	• One size ¾" (1.9 cm) magnetic snap (I use Prym-Dritz brand)
	• 1 spool coordinating all-purpose thread (I use Coats Dual Duty XP)
	See Basic Tools Needed for Each Project (page 14).

- -

ADDITIONAL TOOL NEEDED	• Hand sewing needle

Follow these instructions to make either size bag. Any measurement changes will be noted in the specific step.

1 CUT OUT THE PATTERN PIECES.

From the pattern sheet included with this book, cut out

• Main/inside pocket panel
• Handle
• Peltex handle template

2 CUT OUT ALL OF THE PIECES FROM THE FABRIC.

a. Fold the fabrics in half lengthwise, **Wrong** sides together, matching the selvage edges*.

From the exterior print fabric

• Cut 2 main panels on the fold*

From the coordinating exterior solid

• Cut 4 handles

b. Using a ruler and fabric marker, measure and mark the dimensions below directly onto the **Right** side of the fabric. Then, cut along the marked lines.

• Cut 2 ruffles for small bag: 8" (20.3 cm) wide x 27" (68.6 cm) long
OR
• Cut 2 ruffles for large bag: 8" (20.3 cm) wide x 30" (76.2 cm) long

From the lining fabric

• Cut 2 main panels on the fold
• Cut 2 inside pocket panels on the fold (fold the main/inside pocket panel pattern piece back at the top dashed line)

c. Measure and mark the dimensions below directly onto the **Right** side of the fabric. Then, cut along the marked lines.

• Cut 2 false bottom panels for small bag: $4\frac{1}{2}$" (11.4 cm) wide x $18\frac{1}{4}$" (46.4 cm) long
OR
• Cut 2 false bottom panels for large bag: $4\frac{1}{2}$" (11.4 cm) wide x $21\frac{3}{4}$" (55.2 cm) long

Plus

• Cut 2 cell phone pocket panels: 5" (12.7 cm) wide x $5\frac{1}{2}$" (14 cm) long
• Cut 2 tab closures: $3\frac{1}{2}$" (8.9 cm) wide x 5" (12.7 cm) long

From the fusible interfacing

d. Open up one of the lining main panels and inside pocket panels to use as full-size pattern pieces.

• Cut 2 main panels
• Cut 1 inside pocket panel

e. Use the pattern piece provided and

• Cut 4 handles

f. Measure and mark these dimensions onto a single layer of interfacing. Then, cut along the marked lines.
- Cut 1 cell phone pocket panel: 5" (12.7 cm) wide x 5½" (14 cm) long
- Cut 2 tab closures: 3½" (8.9 cm) wide x 5" (12.7 cm) long

From the fusible fleece
- Cut 2 main panels on the fold

From the fusible Peltex
g. To cut the Peltex for the handles, trace around the template and cut along the marked lines.
- Cut 4 Peltex handles

h. Measure and mark these dimensions directly onto the Peltex, then cut along the marked lines.
- Cut 2 false bottom inserts for small bag: 3¼" (8.3 cm) wide x 17¼" (43.8 cm) long
OR
- Cut 2 false bottom inserts for large bag: 3¼" (8.3 cm) wide x 20¾" (52.7 cm) long

---

3 APPLY THE FUSIBLE INTERFACING AND FLEECE.
Note: See page 172 for interfacing application tips.

a. Place the fusible side of the interfacing main panel onto the **Wrong** side of the first exterior main panel. Using a damp pressing cloth,* fuse the interfacing in place. Turn the panel over and press it again, making sure there are no puckers.

b. Repeat step 3a to fuse the corresponding interfacing pieces to the second exterior main panel, one cell phone pocket, one inside pocket panel, all four handles, and both tab closures.

c. Place the fusible side of one fleece main panel onto the **Wrong** side of the first lining main panel. Fuse it in place. Turn the panel over and press it again, making sure there are no puckers. Repeat to fuse the other fleece panel to the second lining main panel.

d. Place the fusible side (without the protective film) of the first Peltex handle onto the *interfaced* side of the first handle. Center the Peltex and fuse it in place. Repeat to fuse the first side of each Peltex handle to the other three handle pieces.

---

4 MAKE AND ATTACH THE CELL PHONE POCKET TO THE LINING MAIN PANEL.
a. Place the cell phone pocket panels **Right** sides together, matching the edges, and pin them in place.

b. Stitch a ½" (1.3 cm) seam completely around the panels, leaving a 2" (5.1 cm) opening centered on one long side. Backstitch* at each end.

c. Trim* all four corners in the seam allowance,* being careful not to clip your stitching.

d. Turn the pocket **Right** side out through the opening. Use a turning tool* to gently push out the corners. Press the pocket flat. Fold each edge of the opening ½" (1.3 cm) in toward the **Wrong** side. Press and pin the edges together.

e. Topstitch* ¼" (0.6 cm) from the top finished edge. Backstitch at each end.

f. Fold the pocket in half lengthwise, **Right** sides together, and gently press a crease on the fold. Pin the edges ½" (1.3 cm) from the fold along both the top and the bottom of the panel.

g. To make a pleat at the bottom of the pocket, start at the bottom edge and stitch up along the crease 1½" (3.8 cm) in length, using a ½" (1.3 cm) seam from the folded edge. Backstitch at each end. Center the pleat that forms on the back of the pocket evenly on each side of the seam and press it flat. Leave the top edge pinned to form a temporary pleat. The pin will be removed after the pocket has been stitched in place in step 4j.

h. Fold one lining main panel in half, matching the side edges, and gently press a crease on the fold. Open the panel. Using your ruler and fabric marker, measure 6" (15.2 cm) (for small bag) or 8" (20.3 cm) (for large bag) up from the bottom edge and then 3" (7.6 cm) to the right of the center crease, and make a mark.

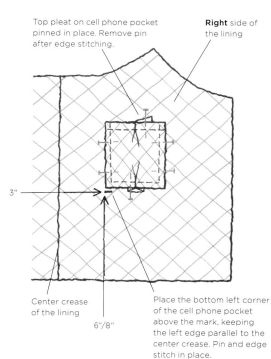

Figure 1

Top pleat on cell phone pocket pinned in place. Remove pin after edge stitching.

Right side of the lining

3"

Center crease of the lining

6"/8"

Place the bottom left corner of the cell phone pocket above the mark, keeping the left edge parallel to the center crease. Pin and edge stitch in place.

i. Place the bottom left corner of the cell phone pocket above the mark and pin the pocket in place, keeping the left edge of the pocket parallel to the center crease on the main panel.

j. Edge stitch* the pocket in place, stitching down each side and across the bottom. Backstitch at each end. Remove the pin at the top edge to release the temporary pleat.

5 **MAKE AND ATTACH THE INSIDE POCKET TO THE LINING MAIN PANEL.**

a. Place the pocket panels **Right** sides together, matching the raw edges. Pin one long edge.

b. Stitch a ½" (1.3 cm) seam across the pinned edge. Backstitch at each end.

c. Turn the pocket **Right** side out, and press. Topstitch ¼" (0.6 cm) from the top finished edge. Backstitch at each end.

d. Match the remaining 3 edges of the pocket and pin them together. Machine baste* ¼" (0.6 cm) from the edges.

e. Fold the pocket in half, matching the side edges, and gently press a crease on the fold.

f. Place the pocket on the lining main panel with the cell phone pocket already attached. Match the side and bottom edges and the center creases, and pin in place.

g. Machine baste ¼" (0.6 cm) from the sides and bottom edges of the panels to hold them in place.

h. Stitch down the center crease to divide the pocket into 2 sections. Backstitch at each end.

Please set the lining panel aside for now.

- -

6 MAKE, GATHER, AND ATTACH THE RUFFLES TO THE EXTERIOR MAIN PANELS.

a. Mark the placement for the ruffle on the exterior main panels by first finding the center of the panel. Fold the first main panel in half lengthwise, matching the side edges, and gently press a crease along the fold. Open the panel.

b. Measure and mark ½" (1.3 cm) down from the top edge on the center crease and then 2¾" (7 cm) up from the bottom edge.

c. Repeat steps 6a and 6b to mark the placement for the ruffle on the second main panel.

d. Fold one short end of the first ruffle ¼" (0.6 cm) under toward the **Wrong** side, and press.

e. Fold it under again ¼" (0.6 cm) toward the **Wrong** side, and press. Pin and then edge stitch along the inner folded edge.

f. Repeat steps 6d and 6e to hem the other short end of the first ruffle.

g. Fold the first ruffle in half lengthwise with **Right** sides together, matching the long edges, and pin. Stitch a ½" (1.3 cm) seam along the pinned edges. Backstitch at each end. Press the seam allowances open.

h. Turn the ruffle **Right** side out and press flat, placing the seam at the center back.

i. Using the longest stitch length on your machine, sew a gathering stitch* the length of the ruffle stitching, ¼" (0.6 cm) on each side of the centered seam. Leave about 6" (15.2 cm) of thread on each end of both stitching lines. *Do not backstitch.*

j. Gently pull both bobbin threads on these two stitch lines at the same time, beginning the gathering process.

k. Gather the ruffle, distributing the gathers evenly, until the ruffle measures 8¾" (22.2 cm) long (for short bag) or 11" (27.9 cm) long (for large bag).

l. Secure the ends of the gathering lines by inserting a straight pin at each end of the ruffle. Starting at the top of the ruffle, take both ends of the threads and put them together. Then make a figure 8 a few times around the top and bottom of the pin. Repeat to secure the bottom of the ruffle.

m. Pin the top edge of the ruffle at the top mark on the exterior main panel, matching the centered seam on the back of the ruffle with the center crease on the main panel. The bottom edge of the ruffle will be even with the bottom mark on the main panel. Then, pin the gathered ruffle along the center crease.

n. Sew the ruffle to the main panel with two lines of stitching. Stitch just inside each gathering stitch line. The stitching lines will be ⅛" (0.3 cm) apart. Backstitch at each end.

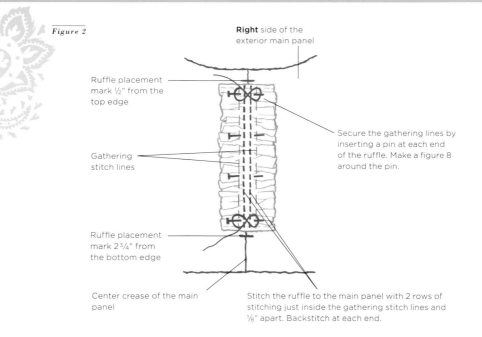

Figure 2

Right side of the exterior main panel

Ruffle placement mark ½" from the top edge

Secure the gathering lines by inserting a pin at each end of the ruffle. Make a figure 8 around the pin.

Gathering stitch lines

Ruffle placement mark 2¾" from the bottom edge

Center crease of the main panel

Stitch the ruffle to the main panel with 2 rows of stitching just inside the gathering stitch lines and ⅛" apart. Backstitch at each end.

o. Remove the pins and then the gathering stitches by pulling the bobbin and top threads completely out from the ruffle.

p. Repeat steps 6a through 6o to make and attach the second ruffle to the second exterior main panel.

7 MAKE THE EXTERIOR OF THE BAG.

a. Place the exterior main panels **Right** sides together, matching the side and bottom edges, and pin in place.

b. Stitch a ½" (1.3 cm) seam down both sides and across the bottom of the panels. Backstitch at each end. Press the seam allowances open.

c. Make a gusset* at the first bottom corner of the exterior panels by matching the side and bottom seams to form a triangle in the corner. Pin the seams together.

d. Measure and mark 1¾" (4.4 cm) from the point along the seam line. Draw a straight line across the corner at the mark. (See Figure 3 on page 150.)

e. Stitch along the marked line and backstitch at each end. Trim the corner to create a ½" (1.3 cm) seam allowance.

f. Repeat steps 7c through 7e to make the gusset in the opposite corner.

g. Stay stitch* ⅜" (1 cm) along the center curve at the top edge of each main panel. Clip* into the seam allowance every ½" to ¾" (1.3 cm to 1.9 cm), being careful not to clip past the stay-stitching line.

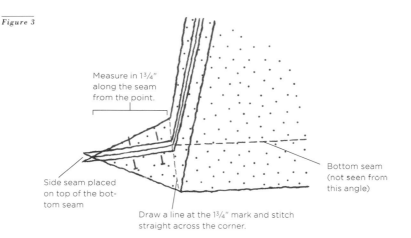

Figure 3

Measure in 1¾"
along the seam
from the point.

Bottom seam
(not seen from
this angle)

Side seam placed
on top of the bot-
tom seam

Draw a line at the 1¾" mark and stitch
straight across the corner.

h. Turn the exterior of the bag **Right** side out and use a turning tool to gently push out the corners.

Please set the exterior aside for now.

 MAKE THE LINING.

a. Repeat steps 7a and 7b to make the lining, leaving an 8" (20.3 cm) opening centered along the bottom edge.

b. Repeat steps 7c through 7g to complete the lining.

MAKE THE HANDLES.

a. On the inside opening of the first handle, clip into the seam allowance every ½" (1.3 cm).

b. Remove the protective film from the Peltex. Gently push the inside edges of the handle toward the fusible side of the Peltex; using only the tip of your iron, press the fabric to the Peltex to fuse it in place. ***Note: Be careful not to touch your iron to the fusible area of the Peltex.***

c. Repeat steps 9a and 9b to clip and press the inside edges of the second handle.

d. Place the first two handles **Right** sides together, matching all of the edges. Pin across the top curved edge.

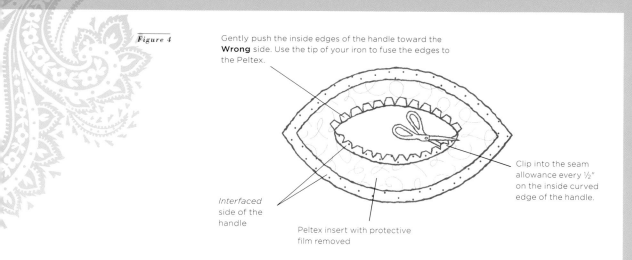

Figure 4

Gently push the inside edges of the handle toward the **Wrong** side. Use the tip of your iron to fuse the edges to the Peltex.

Clip into the seam allowance every ½" on the inside curved edge of the handle.

Interfaced side of the handle

Peltex insert with protective film removed

e. Stitch a ½" (1.3 cm) seam along the top pinned edge, stopping and starting at the end of the Peltex insert. Backstitch at each end. This will leave ½" (1.3 cm) unstitched at each end of the handle.

f. Turn the handle **Right** side out, being sure to tuck the seam allowances between the Peltex inserts. Align the handles so the curves match along both inner and outer edges.

g. Press the handles together, fusing the Peltex in place. There will be ½" (1.3 cm) of fabric extending from either side of the top edge. Edge stitch completely around the inside edges and backstitch at each end. This piece will now be referred to as a single handle.

h. Match the bottom edges of the handle and pin them together.

i. Repeat steps 9a through 9h to make the second handle.

Figure 5

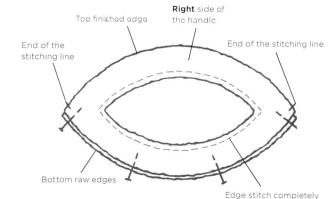

Top finished edge

Right side of the handle

End of the stitching line

End of the stitching line

Bottom raw edges

Edge stitch completely around the inside edges.

10 MAKE THE TAB CLOSURES AND ATTACH THE MAGNETIC SNAP.

a. Find the center of the tab to mark the placement for the magnetic snap. Fold the tab closure in half with the *interfaced* sides together, matching the long [5" (12.7cm)] edges. Gently press a crease and open up the tab.

b. On the **Right** side of the tab closure, using your ruler and fabric marker, measure $1\frac{3}{4}$" (4.4 cm) down on the center crease from one short edge and make a mark.

c. Center the female half of the magnetic snap over the $1\frac{3}{4}$" (4.4 cm) mark and install the snap following the manufacturer's instructions.

d. Fold the tab closure in half, **Right** sides together, matching the short edges. Pin in place. Stitch a $\frac{1}{2}$" (1.3 cm) seam along each side edge, leaving the top edges unstitched. Backstitch at each end.

e. Trim the two corners, being careful not to cut the stitching. Turn the tab closure **Right** side out. Use a turning tool to gently push out the corners, and press the tab flat.

f. Fold each side of the opening under $\frac{1}{2}$" (1.3 cm) toward the **Wrong** side and pin the edges together. You will sew this edge closed when you attach the tab closure in step 11n.

g. Starting at the top, edge stitch down both sides and across the bottom of the tab. Backstitch at each end.

h. Repeat steps 10a through 10g to make the other tab closure with the male half of the magnetic snap.

11 ATTACH THE HANDLES AND TAB CLOSURES AND COMPLETE THE BAG.

a. Place the pinned bottom edges of the first handle **Right** sides together with the center clipped curve of one exterior main panel. Ease the edges around the curve and pin them in place. (See Figure 6 on next page.)

b. Machine baste a $\frac{3}{8}$" (1 cm) seam along the pinned edges.

c. Repeat steps 11a and 11b to baste the second handle to the other exterior main panel.

d. With the lining **Wrong** side out and the exterior **Right** side out, slip the lining over the exterior, sandwiching the handles between the panels. Ease and pin the lining to the first handle.

e. Stitch a $\frac{1}{2}$" (1.3 cm) seam along the pinned edges, starting and stopping $\frac{1}{2}$" (1.3 cm) from each end. Backstitch at each end. You will be stitching through the exterior main panel, two layers of the handle fabric (not the Peltex), and the lining main panel. Use the edge of the Peltex as a guide for your stitching. There will be $\frac{1}{2}$" (1.3 cm) of the main panels extending from each end of the finished handles.

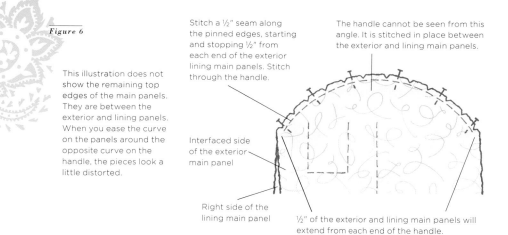

Figure 6

This illustration does not show the remaining top edges of the main panels. They are between the exterior and lining panels. When you ease the curve on the panels around the opposite curve on the handle, the pieces look a little distorted.

Stitch a ½" seam along the pinned edges, starting and stopping ½" from each end of the exterior lining main panels. Stitch through the handle.

The handle cannot be seen from this angle. It is stitched in place between the exterior and lining main panels.

Interfaced side of the exterior main panel

Right side of the lining main panel

½" of the exterior and lining main panels will extend from each end of the handle.

f. Repeat steps 11d and 11e to attach the second handle to the other side of the exterior and lining panels.

g. Pull out the remaining top edges of the exterior and lining main panels on each side of both handles. Match the top edges, including the ½" (1.3 cm) that extends past each side of the handles, and pin the edges together.

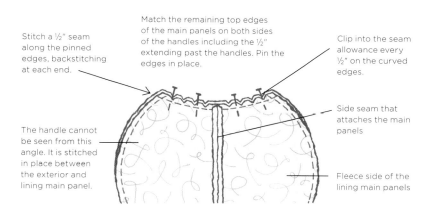

Figure 7

Stitch a ½" seam along the pinned edges, backstitching at each end.

Match the remaining top edges of the main panels on both sides of the handles including the ½" extending past the handles. Pin the edges in place.

Clip into the seam allowance every ½" on the curved edges.

The handle cannot be seen from this angle. It is stitched in place between the exterior and lining main panel.

Side seam that attaches the main panels

Fleece side of the lining main panels

h. Starting at the stitching line that attaches the first handle, sew a ½" (1.3 cm) seam along the pinned edges and across the side seam, stopping at the second handle on the other side. Backstitch at each end. Repeat this step to sew the pinned edges across the other side seam.

i. Clip into the seam allowance every ½" (1.3 cm) on all the curved edges, being careful not to clip your stitching.

j. Turn the bag **Right** side out through the 8″ (20.3 cm) opening in the bottom of the lining. Push the lining down inside the exterior, and press.

k. Edge stitch around the top finished edge of the bag, including the top curved edges of the handles. Backstitch at each end.

l. Measure and mark 6¼″ (15.9 cm) in along the bottom edge of the handle lining to mark the center for the tab placement.

m. Center the top pinned end of the first tab closure over the mark and allow the tab to overlap the first handle by ¼″ (0.6 cm). Make sure the magnetic snap faces out and pin the tab in place. Repeat to attach the second tab. ***Note: The tab closure snaps together as it hangs down inside the bag.***

n. Edge stitch both handles along the bottom curved edges, catching the tops of both tab closures, securing them in place. Backstitch at each end.

o. Pull the bottom of the lining out from the exterior. Fold each edge of the opening under ½″ (1.3 cm), and press. Pin and then edge stitch the opening closed. Push the lining back inside the exterior of the bag and press.

MAKE THE FALSE BOTTOM.

a. Place the false bottom panels **Right** sides together, matching the raw edges, and pin in place.

b. Stitch a ½″ (1.3 cm) seam down both long edges and across one short end. Backstitch at each end.

c. Trim the corners in the seam allowance, being careful not to clip your stitching.

d. Turn the false bottom **Right** side out. Use a turning tool to gently push out the corners, and press.

e. Remove the protective film from the Peltex inserts and place them together, matching the edges. Machine baste ¼″ (0.6 cm) from the edges completely around the inserts.

f. Place the Peltex inserts inside the false bottom. You may need to gently bow the inserts when tucking them inside the fabric.

g. Fold each side on the open end of the false bottom under ½″ (1.3 cm). Pin the edges and then slipstitch* the opening closed. Use your iron to fuse the panels together.

h. Topstitch ¼″ (0.6 cm) from the edges completely around the false bottom. Place the false bottom inside your bag to lend added support.

Your Miss Maven Ruffled Handbag is complete! Now show off your flirtatious side by going out and stealing all the attention.

12

Take Flight Handbag/ Shoulder Bag

The big peacock tail detail on this bag will let you strut your creative stuff! Modeled after '60s travel bags, this plumed tote has modern, simple lines and a convenient top zipper. Two strap lengths will suit your various needs. The hardest part of making this bag just might be choosing your fabric feathers!

FINISHED SIZE	**Handbag**
	13″ (33 cm) wide across the top [17″ (43.2 cm) wide across the bottom] x 11″ (27.9 cm) tall [or 16½″ (42 cm) tall with the handles] x 4″ (10.2 cm) deep
	Shoulder bag
	13″ (33 cm) wide across the top [17″ (43.2 cm) wide across the bottom] x 11″ (27.9 cm) tall [or 18½″ (47 cm) tall with long handles] x 4″ (10.2 cm) deep

= =

FABRICS

- 1½ yd (1.37 m) of 54″ (137 cm) wide mid-weight Home Dec solid for the exterior side panels, top panels, handles, and lining
- ½ yd (46 m) of 54″ (137 cm) wide second mid-weight Home Dec solid for the exterior main panels
- ⅜ yd (0.34 m) of 44″ (112 cm) wide light- to mid-weight print for 6 petals
- ⅜ yd (0.34 m) of 44″ (112 cm) wide light- to mid-weight coordinating print for 8 petals
- ½ yd (0.46 m) of 44″ (112 cm) wide light- to mid-weight solid fabric for the bias trim

- -

OTHER SUPPLIES

- 2¾ yd (2.51 m) of 20″ (50.8 cm) wide fusible woven interfacing (I use Shape Flex SF-101 by Pellon)
- 1¼ yd (1.14 m) of 20″ (50.8 cm) wide single-sided fusible Peltex by Pellon or a similar extra-heavy stabilizer
- ⅛ yd (0.11 m) of 44″ (112 cm) wide fusible fleece (I use fusible Thermolam Plus by Pellon)
- One 22″ (55.9 cm) coordinating zipper (I use Coats brand)
- 1 spool coordinating all-purpose thread (I use Coats Dual Duty XP)

See Basic Tools Needed for Each Project (page 14).

- -

ADDITIONAL TOOLS NEEDED

- Masking tape
- Marker
- Seam ripper
- Zipper foot for your sewing machine
- Hand sewing needle

Follow these instructions to make the bag with either size handle. Any measurement changes will be noted in the specific step.

---

1 CUT OUT THE PATTERN PIECES.

From the pattern sheet included with this book, cut out
- Main panel
- Side panel
- Petal A
- Petal B
- Petal C
- Petal D

---

2 CUT OUT ALL OF THE PIECES FROM THE FABRIC.

Tip: Using a piece of masking tape and a marker, write the name of each panel on the tape and place it on the individual fabric pieces to identify them.

a. Use a single layer of fabric and fold each selvage edge* 9" (22.9 cm) in toward the **Wrong** side.

From the first solid fabric
- Cut 2 main panels on the fold*
- Cut 4 side panels on the fold

b. Open the fabric. Using a ruler and fabric marker, measure and mark the dimensions below directly onto the **Right** side of a single layer of fabric. Then, cut along the marked lines.
- Cut 4 top panels: $2^5/8$" (6.7 cm) wide x 21" (53.3 cm) long
- Cut 2 bottom panels: 5" (12.7 cm) wide x 18" (45.7 cm) long
- Cut 2 pocket panels: 13" (33 cm) wide x $9^1/2$" (24.1 cm) long
- Cut 2 short handles to make the handbag: $4^1/2$" (11.4 cm) wide x $15^1/2$" (39.4 cm) long
OR
- Cut 2 long handles to make the shoulder bag: $4^1/2$" (11.4 cm) wide x $19^1/2$" (49.5 cm) long

From the coordinating solid exterior fabric
- Cut 2 main panels on the fold

c. Fold the petal fabrics in half lengthwise, **Wrong** sides together, matching the selvage edges.

From the first light- to mid-weight print fabric
- Cut 2 petal A's
- Cut 4 petal C's

From the second light- to mid-weight print fabric

- Cut 4 petal B's
- Cut 4 petal D's

From the light- to mid-weight solid for the bias trim

d. Set aside the fabric. You will cut and attach the bias* strips in step 4a.

e. Open the cut exterior and lining fabric panels. Use the panels as full-size pattern pieces to cut out the interfacing and Peltex.

From the fusible interfacing

- Cut 2 main panels
- Cut 2 side panels
- Cut 2 top panels
- Cut 2 bottom panels
- Cut 2 handles
- Cut 1 pocket panel

f. To cut the petals from the interfacing, fold the cut edge of the interfacing 6" (15.2 cm) over with the fusible sides together.

- Cut 2 petal A's

Fold the fusible interfacing 6" (15.2 cm) in again

- Cut 2 petal B's
- Cut 2 petal C's

Fold the fusible interfacing 6" (15.2 cm) in again

- Cut 2 petal B's
- Cut 2 petal C's

Fold the fusible interfacing 6" (15.2 cm) in again

- Cut 4 petal D's

From the fusible Peltex

- Cut 2 main panels
- Cut 2 side panels

g. Using your ruler and marker, measure and mark the following dimensions directly onto a single layer of Peltex. Then, cut along the marked lines.

- Cut 2 bottom panels: 4" (10.2 cm) wide x 17" (43.2 cm) long

h. On each of the Peltex main and side panels, measure and mark ½" (1.3 cm) in around all the edges. Draw a line connecting the marks. Use your scissors and cut along the marked lines. This will help reduce bulk in the seam allowances*.

From the fusible fleece

- Cut 2 top panels: 1½" (3.8 cm) wide x 20" (50.8 cm) long
- Cut 2 short handle inserts: 1⅛" (2.9 cm) wide x 15½" (39.4 cm) long
OR
- Cut 2 long handle inserts: 1⅛" (2.9 cm) wide x 19½" (49.5 cm) long

3 APPLY FUSIBLE INTERFACINGS.

Note: See page 172 for interfacing application tips.

a. Place the **Wrong** side of each petal onto the fusible side of each corresponding interfacing piece. Using a damp pressing cloth,* fuse the interfacing in place. Turn the panel over and press it again, making sure there are no puckers.

b. Center the Peltex panel on the **Wrong** side of the first exterior main panel leaving ½"(1.3 cm) of the main panel exposed around the edges. Then, place the fusible side of the interfacing onto the Peltex and fuse it in place, sealing the edges and securing the Peltex. Repeat to attach the Peltex and interfacing to the second main panel. Set aside.

c. Repeat step 3b to attach the Peltex and interfacing on the **Wrong** side of two of the side panels. They will now be referred to as exterior side panels.

d. Place the 2 Peltex bottom panels with the fusible sides together. Match the edges and fuse in place.

e. Repeat step 3b to attach the Peltex and interfacing to one of the bottom panels. This will be referred to as the exterior bottom panel.

f. Repeat step 3b to attach the fusible fleece and interfacing to two of the top panel pieces, and set aside. These will now be referred to as the exterior top panels.

g. Place the fusible side of the interfacing on the **Wrong** side of both handles and one of the bottom and pocket panels. Fuse in place and set aside.

4 MAKE AND ATTACH THE BIAS STRIPS AROUND THE PETALS.

a. Follow the instructions in Glossary & Techniques (page 171) to cut 10 to 15 bias strips [1" (2.6 cm) wide] and attach them to make 270" (6.86 m) of bias trim.

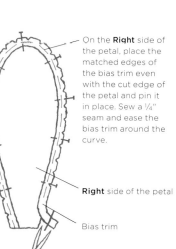

Figure 1

Clip V-shaped notches into the seam allowance every ½" to ¾" around the curved edges. Be careful not to clip the stitching.

Cut off bias trim even with bottom of the petal.

On the **Right** side of the petal, place the matched edges of the bias trim even with the cut edge of the petal and pin it in place. Sew a ¼" seam and ease the bias trim around the curve.

Right side of the petal

Bias trim

b. Fold the bias trim in half lengthwise, **Wrong** sides together, and press along the folded edge. Machine baste* ¼" (0.6 cm) from the matched edges.

c. On the **Right** side of the first petal, place the matched edges of the bias trim even with the cut edge of the petal and pin it in place. Stitch the trim ¼" (0.6 cm) from the cut edge, easing it around the curved edge of the petal. Backstitch* at each end.

d. Clip* V-shaped notches every $\frac{1}{2}$" to $\frac{3}{4}$" (1.3 cm to 1.9 cm) around the curved edges into the seam allowance. Be careful not to clip the stitching.

e. Fold the clipped edges under toward the *interfaced* side of the petal, and press. Cut off the excess bias binding even with the bottom edge of the petal.

f. Repeat steps 4c through 4e to attach the trim to the other 13 petals.

5 ATTACH THE PETALS TO THE EXTERIOR MAIN PANELS.

a. Divide the petals into 2 sets. On each exterior main panel, there are 2 petal D's, C's, and B's, and 1 petal A centered in the middle.

b. Place the first main panel **Right** side up. Use a fabric marker and make a mark $2\frac{3}{4}$" (7 cm) in from each corner along the bottom edge.

c. Using the first set of petals, place a petal D on the inside of each mark and match the bottom edge of the petals with the bottom edge of the main panel. Pin them in place.

d. Stitch-in-the-ditch* all the way around the petals on the seam between the petal and bias trim. Backstitch at each end.

e. Repeat steps 5b through 5d using the following placement measurements, measuring in from the bottom corners.
• Petal C's: $5\frac{3}{4}$" (15 cm)
• Petal B's: $6\frac{7}{8}$" (17 cm)
• Petal A: centered on the main panel

f. Repeat steps 5b through 5e to attach the second set of petals to the second main panel.

Please set aside for now.

6 MAKE THE HANDLES.
Note: Follow these instructions if making either the short or the long handle.

a. Fold the first handle in half lengthwise, *interfaced* sides together, and press a crease along the folded edge.

b. Open up the handle. Fold the long edges in to meet the center crease, and press.

c. Slip the fleece handle insert under one of the folded edges, fusible side up.

d. Fold the handle in half again at the center crease, enclosing the raw edges. Pin and press the handle to secure the fleece.

e. Edge stitch* along both folded edges and backstitch at each end.

f. Topstitch* $\frac{1}{4}$" (0.6 cm) from the edge, stitching on each side of the handle for detail. Backstitch at each end.

g. Repeat steps 6a through 6f to make the second handle.

7

ATTACH THE HANDLES TO THE MAIN PANELS.

a. On the first exterior main panel, measure and mark 4″ (10.2 cm) in from each corner along the top edge.

b. Place the inside edge of the end of one handle to the outside of the first mark, matching the raw edges. Pin it in place.

c. Machine baste a 1/4″ (0.6 cm) seam across the end of the handle to secure it in place on the main panel.

d. Place the other end of the handle to the outside of the second mark, being careful not to twist the handle. Pin and machine baste it in place.

e. Repeat steps 7a through 7d to attach the second handle to the second main panel.

Please set the main panels aside for now.

8

INSTALL THE ZIPPER ON THE TOP PANELS.

a. Place the exterior top panels **Right** sides together, matching the edges, and pin across one long edge. Measure 1″ (2.5 cm) in from each side edge along the pinned edge and make a mark. Then, stitch a 5/8″ (1.6 cm) seam from each side edge, stopping at the 1″ (2.5 cm) marks. Backstitch at each end.

b. Machine baste a 5/8″ (1.6 cm) seam across the rest of the long edge, from the end of one stitching line to the other. Press the seam allowance open.

c. Place the top of the zipper at the beginning of the basting stitch, centering the coils over the seam. Pin it in place.

d. Using the zipper foot on your machine, start at the top of one side of the zipper and stitch 3/8″ (1 cm) from the zipper coils down one long side of the tape. Pivot* and stitch 3/4″ (1.9 cm) across the end of the zipper; pivot again, stitch down the other long side. Then, pivot and stitch across the top of the zipper. Backstitch at each end.

e. Using your seam ripper, remove the basting stitches to open the seam so your zipper can function.

9 ATTACH THE EXTERIOR SIDE PANELS TO THE TOP PANELS.

a. Place the exterior side and top panels **Right** sides together, matching the short ends on each side of the top panel. Pin each end in place. Stitch a ½" (1.3 cm) seam across each pinned edge. Backstitch at each end. Press the seam allowances toward the side panels.

b. Topstitch ¼" (0.6 cm) from the seam that attaches the side panel to the top panel, catching the seam allowances underneath.

Figure 2

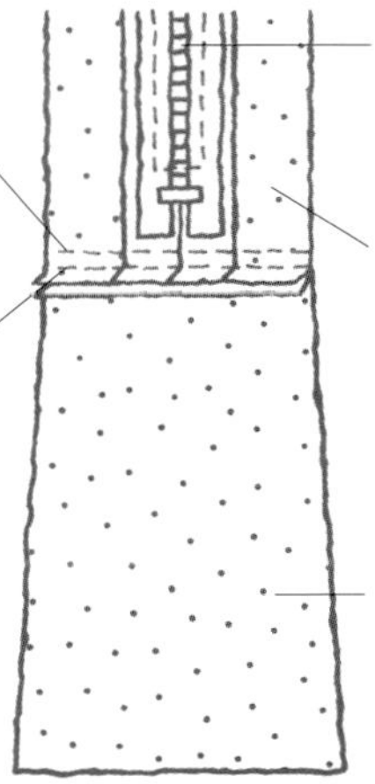

Seam that attaches the side and top panels with the seam allowances pressed toward the side panel

Zipper

Interfaced side of the top panel

Topstitch ¼" from the seam that attaches the side and top panels.

Interfaced side of the side panel

10 ATTACH THE MAIN PANELS TO THE TOP/SIDE PANEL.

a. Fold the top panel in half, matching the short ends. Place a straight pin at the top of the folded edge on each side of the top panel to mark the center. Repeat to mark the top center of each main panel.

b. Place the first main and top panels **Right** sides together, matching the marked center of each panel. Pin the panels together across the top edge of the main panel.

c. Stitch a ½" (1.3 cm) seam across the pinned edge, starting and stopping ½" (1.3 cm) in from each side edge of the main panel. Backstitch at each end.

d. Clip into the seam allowance at each end of the stitching on the top panel only.

e. Turn the top panel at the first clip and match it to the side edges on the main panel, pinning them in place. Repeat to pin the other side edges together.

f. Starting at the clip on the top panel, stitch a ½" (1.3 cm) seam down both sides, stopping ½" (1.3 cm) up from the bottom edges. Backstitch at each end.

g. Repeat steps 10b through 10f to attach the second main panel to the other side of the top panel.

h. Trim* the corners in the seam allowance. Make sure not to clip the stitching.

11 ATTACH THE BOTTOM PANEL TO THE MAIN AND SIDE PANELS.

Note: Leave the zipper open for this step so you can turn the bag Right side out.

a. Place one long edge of the bottom panel and the bottom edge of the first main panel **Right** sides together, and pin in place. Stitch a $\frac{1}{2}$" (1.3 cm) seam, starting and stopping $\frac{1}{2}$" (1.3 cm) in from each side edge. Backstitch at each end.

Figure 3

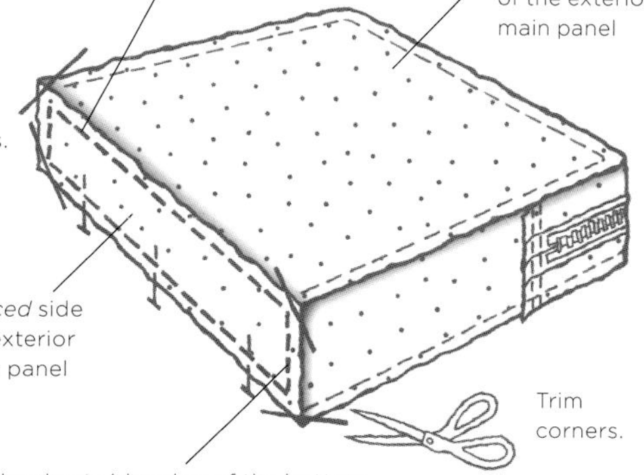

Place the long edge of the bottom panel and bottom edge of the main panel **Right** sides together. Pin and stitch a $\frac{1}{2}$" seam starting and stopping $\frac{1}{2}$" in from each side edge.

Trim corners.

Interfaced side of the exterior main panel

Interfaced side of the exterior bottom panel

Trim corners.

Match the short side edge of the bottom panel with the bottom edge of the side panels. Pin and stitch a $\frac{1}{2}$" seam starting and stopping $\frac{1}{2}$" in from each side edge.

b. Repeat step 11a to attach the other long side of the bottom panel to the bottom edge of the second main panel.

c. Turn the main panel at the side seams and match the bottom edge of one side panel with the short side edge of the bottom panel. Pin in place. Stitch a $\frac{1}{2}$" (1.3 cm) seam across the matched edges, starting and stopping $\frac{1}{2}$" (1.3 cm) in from each side edge. Backstitch at each end.

d. Repeat step 11c to attach the bottom panel to the bottom edge of the second side panel.

e. Trim the corners in the seam allowance, being careful not to cut the stitching.

f. Turn the exterior of the bag **Right** side out. Use a turning tool* to gently push out the corners, and press.

Please set aside for now.

12 MAKE AND ATTACH THE INSIDE POCKET TO THE LINING MAIN PANEL.

a. Place the pocket panels **Right** sides together and pin along the top and side edges. Stitch a $\frac{1}{2}$" (1.3 cm) seam along the pinned edges. Backstitch at each end.

b. Trim the top corners in the seam allowance, making sure not to clip the stitching.

c. Turn the pocket panels **Right** side out and press along the finished edges. Topstitch $\frac{1}{2}$" (1.3 cm) from the top finished edge. Backstitch at each end.

d. Fold the pocket in half lengthwise, matching the side edges. Gently press a crease along the folded edge. Repeat to find the center of one of the lining main panels.

e. Place the pocket onto the **Right** side of the lining main panel, matching the center creases and the bottom edges. Pin it in place. Edge stitch down both side edges and backstitch at each end. Machine baste a ¼" (0.6 cm) seam across the bottom edges.

---

13 MAKE THE LINING.

a. Place the lining top panels **Right** sides together, matching the edges, and pin across one long edge. Stitch a ¾" (1.9 cm) seam, 1" (2.5 cm) in from both short side edges. Backstitch at each end.

b. Fold the edges ¾" (1.9 cm) in toward the **Wrong** side between the stitched ends of the top panels, and press. Then, press the seam allowances open on each end of the panels.

c. Repeat step 8a to attach the side panels to each end of the top panel, using a ⅝" (1.6 cm) seam.

d. Repeat steps 10 and 11 to attach the top/side and bottom panels to the lining main panels. Use a ⅝" (1.6 cm) seam to allow the lining to fit snugly inside the bag. Do *not* turn **Right** side out.

---

14 ATTACH THE LINING TO THE EXTERIOR.

a. With the exterior **Right** side out and the lining **Wrong** side out, slip the lining inside the exterior, matching the side and bottom panels. Match the seams that attach the main and top panels on both the exterior and lining, and pin the first side together.

b. On the exterior of the bag, stitch-in-the-ditch in the seam that attaches the top and main panels. Sew from the outside edge of one end of the handle to the other end of the second handle. Backstitch at each end. You will be sewing through both the exterior and the lining to hold the lining panel in place at the top of the bag.

c. Repeat steps 14a and 14b to match and stitch the seams together on the other side of the bag.

d. Flip each side of the top panel so the lining side is facing out (no need to turn the entire bag lining side out). Place the folded edges of the lining top panels even with the stitching line on the zipper and pin in place along each side. Slipstitch* across each long folded edge. Turn the top of the bag **Right** side out, and press.

Your Flight Bag is complete! With its mod peacock feather design, this bag works well for carrying work and travel necessities or just flying around town!

Glossary & Techniques

Backstitch—This is used to reinforce stitching to help keep it from unraveling. To do this, put your machine in the reverse position and stitch three or four stitches.

Bar tack—To secure a seam or the end of a zipper, use the widest zigzag stitch on your machine and sew a few times in place.

Bias—See *fabric grain*.

Bias trim—Cut the trim on the bias of the fabric by first placing the fabric on a flat surface, **Right** side up. Fold one corner **Right** sides together, matching one selvage edge with one of the cut edges to form a triangle shape. Press a crease on the fold. Open the fabric and cut along the creased edge.

Figure 1

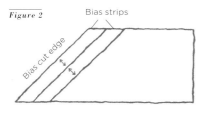

Cut on the fold.

Right side of the fabric

Fold the fabric to form a triangle.

Starting at one end of the cut line, measure over the distance instructed in the project, on the **Right** side of the fabric, and make a mark. Make another mark the same distance on the fabric from the opposite end of the cut line. Match the two marks and draw a line connecting these marks, using a ruler and fabric marker. This will create a bias strip the width needed for your project, parallel to the newly cut edge. Continue to measure and mark bias strips until you have the length called for in the individual project instruction.

Figure 2

Bias strips

Bias cut edge

To join the strips into one long piece, lay the strips perpendicular to each other with **Right** sides together. Stitch across the diagonal edges of the strips with a

½" (1.3 cm) seam. Then, trim the seam allowance to ¼" (0.6 cm) and press the seam allowance open. Trim any small "tails" of the fabric at the seam of the bias strip edges. Repeat until you have joined all of the strips into one long continuous bias strip.

Figure 3

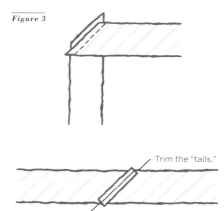

Trim the "tails."

Trim the "tails."

Clip—To clip allows some give in your seam allowance, especially if it is curved, in order to make the seam lie flat and make it easier to turn your project **Right** side out. When clipping, use scissors to cut into the seam allowance only, making cuts up to the stitch line, and taking care not to cut the stitching.

Crosswise grain—See *fabric grain*.

Cut fabric on the fold—To cut a pattern piece on the fold of your fabric, lay the piece even with the folded edge of the fabric and cut following the pattern lines. Once the fabric piece is cut out, open it up to yield one full-size panel.

Edge stitch—An edge stitch is a very narrow stitch, done by machine very close to the finished edge or seam to finish a project, close an opening, or stitch something in place.

Fabric grain—Most fabric is made using a set of fixed lengthwise threads woven at right angles with a set of crosswise threads. Grain indicates the direction of these threads. *Lengthwise grain* (also called *straight of grain*) refers to the lengthwise threads, or the fabric's length parallel to the selvage edge. *Crosswise grain* refers to the crosswise threads, or the fabric's width, and runs across the fabric from selvage to selvage. *Bias* refers

(Continued on page 173)

MANUFACTURER'S NOTES AND INSTRUCTIONS FOR APPLYING INTERFACINGS AND STABILIZERS

1. Fusible fleece (Pellon® Thermolam Plus® Fusible), 100% polyester

a. Always pre-test product and pre-wash fabric.

b. Cut fusible fleece to desired size.

c. Place fleece, fusible side up, on ironing board. Place fabric, **Right** side up, on top of fleece.

d. Fuse. Cover fleece and fabric with a damp pressing cloth. With iron at "wool/steam" setting, press down firmly for 10 to 15 seconds. Repeat, overlapping iron until entire area is fused. For additional loft, use more than one layer of fleece.

e. Machine wash warm and dry medium or dry clean.

2. Fusible woven interfacing (Pellon® Shape-Flex® SF-101), 70% polyester/30% cotton

a. Always pre-test product and pre-wash fabric.

b. SF-101 should also be pre-washed. To do this, put interfacing in warm water for a few minutes. Gently remove and air dry. *Do not* wring or wash in machine as doing so may displace the fusible adhesive.

c. Trim and steam-baste.

• Pin pattern piece to Shape-Flex following grain line arrows; cut. Trim seam allowance to 1/8" (0.3 cm).

• Place fusible side of Shape-Flex onto **Wrong** side of fabric piece. Pin, then steam-baste along edges with tip of iron. Remove pins.

d. Fuse.

• Cover with a damp pressing cloth.

• With iron at "wool/steam" setting, press firmly for a full 10 seconds. Repeat, lifting and slightly overlapping iron until all interfacing is fused.

• Use steam iron with metal sole plate. (Hand-held steamers will not permanently bond interfacing to fabric.)

e. Machine wash warm and dry medium or dry clean.

Tip: Use your damp pressing cloth as a temperature and timing guide. After 10 seconds, pressing cloth should be dry. If not, raise iron temperature or hold iron in place a few seconds longer.

3. Pellon® Peltex® 70 Sew-In Ultra-Firm Stabilizer, 100% polyester

a. Easy to cut with scissors or rotary cutter.

b. Easy to sew, even sandwiched with other fabrics.

c. Will not flatten out or be distorted in steam pressing.

d. Has no grain; can be cut in any direction.

e. Machine wash warm and tumble dry or dry clean.

4. Pellon® Peltex® 71F Single-Sided Fusible Ultra-Firm Stabilizer

a. Always pre-test product and pre-wash fabrics.

b. Place shiny adhesive side up and the **Wrong** side of fabric down and work from fabric side.

c. Use a hot steam iron at "wool" setting. Use a gliding motion and slight pressure to iron Peltex 71F to the fabric.

d. Cover with a damp pressing cloth and press firmly for 10 to 15 seconds.

e. Repeat, lifting and overlapping until all fabric is fused.

f. Remove pressing cloth and iron fabric to eliminate excess moisture.

5. Pellon® Peltex® 72F Double-Sided Fusible Ultra-Firm Stabilizer

a. Always pre-test product and pre-wash fabric.

b. Place clear plastic side of 72F down against the ironing board. Place fabric, **Wrong** side down, against the rough side of the 72F. "Baste" by using a hot iron at "wool" setting and use a gliding motion and slight pressure to iron 72F to the first fabric. Allow to cool.

c. Gently peel off the clear plastic backing. Put this piece, with the white side up, on ironing board.

d. Position the second fabric, **Wrong** side down, on the Peltex. Cover with a damp pressing cloth.

e. With hot iron at "wool" setting, fuse into place by pressing firmly for 10 seconds per area, overlapping slightly each time.

f. Turn fabric "sandwich" over and continue fusing on the other side to permanently bond.

g. Remove pressing cloth and iron fabric to eliminate any excess moisture.

to any diagonal line crossing either the lengthwise or crosswise grain. The *bias fold* refers to the diagonal fold of a rectangle of fabric to align one selvage edge (or an edge cut on the lengthwise grain) with one edge cut on the crosswise grain, producing a 45-degree-angle fold.

Gathering stitch—Using the longest stitch on your machine and a loose bobbin tension enables you to pull the bobbin thread to gather your fabric (do not backstitch at either end).

Gusset—This is a small square or triangular-shaped piece of fabric that is created by placing a side seam flat against a bottom seam or crease and stitching across them. A gusset will make a square bottom where there was only a flat-seamed bottom.

Interfacing—*See Manufacturer's Notes and Instructions for Applying Interfacings and Stabilizers, page 172.*

Lengthwise grain—See *fabric grain.*

Machine baste—A machine basting stitch is used to hold sections of the project in place until you are ready to complete final stitches. Use the longest stitch on your machine, so you can easily remove these basting stitches later. You do *not* have to backstitch at either end of your stitching.

Pivot—Pivoting is used when you reach a corner or any place where you want to turn and continue stitching in a different direction. To pivot, stop stitching with the needle in the down position (keeping the fabric in place in the sewing machine), raise the presser foot, and rotate or move the fabric to continue stitching in a different direction.

Pressing cloth—A pressing cloth is a piece of neutral fabric, placed between the project and the iron to prevent shiny marks or scorching caused by the heat of the iron. You can dampen the pressing cloth when you want to create more steam to help press seams and press out creases in the fabric.

Seam allowance—The seam allowance is the fabric extending from the stitching line to the edge. It can be pressed open or to one side as indicated in the project instructions.

Selvage edge—The narrow, tightly woven finished edge along each side of the lengthwise grain of your fabric.

Slipstitch—Frequently used to join two folded edges, slipstitching is nearly invisible as the thread is slipped under the fabric's fold. You will need a long piece of thread and a sharp needle.

a. To begin, feed one end of the thread through the eye of the needle, doubling the thread back on itself. Match up the cut ends and make a double knot.

b. Insert the needle into the fabric and pull the thread taut, hiding the knot.

c. Insert the needle through a few threads on the other edge of the fabric. Pull the thread through until it is taut.

d. Insert the needle back into the first side, through about 1/2" (1.3 cm) of the fabric, hiding the thread inside a fold. Push the needle through the fabric and again pull the thread taut.

e. Repeat this process until you have stitched your fabric together, keeping even spaces between stitches.

f. To finish, tie off the stitching by making a double knot close to the fabric and cutting the excess threads to free the needle.

Stay stitch—Stay stitching is used in the seam allowance before construction to stabilize curved or slanted edges so the fabric on these edges does not stretch.

Stitch-in-the-ditch—This stitching, done either by machine or by hand as indicated in the pattern instructions, is sewn in the groove formed by the seam. Make sure to line up any seams underneath so both seams will be sewn neatly.

Topstitch—Topstitching is used for several purposes. It finishes your project and gives it a neat appearance; it is used to close openings left after turning a project **Right** side out; and it can be used as a reinforcement stitch by adding another row of stitching to areas that will be used heavily and receive more wear. To topstitch, stitch parallel to an edge or another seam for the distance suggested in the project's instructions.

Transfer lines from pattern piece to fabric piece—On a hard flat surface, using a tracing wheel and wax-free tracing paper, place the tracing paper with the colored side toward the **Right** side of the fabric. Place the pattern piece over the tracing paper. Roll the tracing wheel firmly around or across the line to be transferred. Move the tracing paper to continue with a pattern or, if finished, remove it. The lines will show on the fabric.

Trim in corners—This is a finishing technique used to add shape and definition to the corners of the project. Use scissors to cut off the tip of the corner in the seam allowance to eliminate bulk. Be careful not to cut into the project or stitching. Once you turn the project **Right** side out, the corners will have a neat, squared-off look.

Trim in seam allowances—This technique reduces bulk around curved seams so they will lie flat when you turn the project **Right** side out. Use your scissors to cut off most of the excess fabric in the seam allowances. Be sure to press out these areas once you have turned them **Right** side out.

Turning tool—A turning tool is a pointed object, such as a closed pair of scissors, that can be used to push out the corners on a project after you have turned it **Right** side out. Specially made turning tools, usually constructed of plastic or wood, are available at sewing and fabric stores. When using a turning tool, push out the corners gently, especially if you are working with delicate, lightweight fabric.

Fabric Reference Guide

COSMO BAG (PAGE 19)

Shoulder bag

Exterior :
AB-25 Honeycomb
Color: Rust
From the Midwest Modern collection

Bands/handles:
AB-45
Color: Gold
From the quilting-weight Solids collection

Lining:
AB-32 Fresh Poppies
Color: Rose
From the Midwest Modern collection

Handbag

Exterior:
AB-34 Wildflowers
Color: Rose
From the Daisy Chain collection

Bands/handles:
AB-35 Mosaic
Color: Rose
From the Daisy Chain collection

SEEN ON PAGE 8

Handbag (bottom left)

Main panel:
AB-51 Water Bouquet
Color: Mist
From the Love collection

Band/handles:
AB-47 Cypress Paisley
Color: Blush
From the Love collection

Shoulder bag (bottom right)

Main panel:
AB-52 Bali Gate
Color: Pink
From the Love collection

Band/handles:
AB-50 Bliss Bouquet
Color: Emerald
From the Love collection

REVERSIBLE EVERYDAY SHOPPER (PAGE 31)

Bag 1

Exterior:
HDABS-13 Coreopsis
Color: Peach
From the August Fields collection

Pockets/handles/reversible side:
HDABS-10 Sunrise
Color: Seafoam
From the August Fields collection

Bag 2

Exterior:
HDABS-09 Knot Garden
Color: Olive
From the August Fields collection

Pockets/handles/reversible side:
HDABS-11 Graceful Vine
Color: Moss
From the August Fields collection

Bag 3

Exterior:
HDABS-10 Sunrise
Color: Seafoam
From the August Fields collection

Pockets/handles/reversible side:
HDABS-15 Full Bloom
Color: Forest
From the August Fields collection

ORIGAMI BAG SET (PAGE 41)

X-small bag

Exterior A:
HDABS-12 Fresh Start
Color: Spruce
From the August Fields collection

Exterior B:
HDABS-13 Coreopsis
Color: Green
From the August Fields collection

Lining:
HDABS-09 Knot Garden
Color: Grey
From the August Fields collection

Mini bag

Exterior A:
HDABS-12 Fresh Start
Color: Grey
From the August Fields collection

Exterior B:
HDABS-10 Sunrise
Color: Grey
From the August Fields collection

Lining:
HDABS-09 Knot Garden
Color: Grey
From the August Fields collection

Small bag

Exterior A:
HDABS-13 Coreopsis
Color: Green
From the August Fields collection

Exterior B:
HDABS-12 Fresh Start
Color: Spruce
From the August Fields collection

Lining:
HDABS-09 Knot Garden
Color: Grey
From the August Fields collection

Medium bag

Exterior A:
HDABS-10 Sunrise
Color: Grey
From the August Fields collection

Exterior B:
HDABS-12 Fresh Start
Color: Grey
From the August Fields collection

Lining:
HDABS-09 Knot Garden
Color: Grey
From the August Fields collection

Large bag

Exterior A:
HDABS-13 Coreopsis
Color: Spruce
From the August Fields collection

Exterior B:
HDABS-13 Coreopsis
Color: Green
From the August Fields collection

Lining:
HDABS-09 Knot Garden
Color: Celery
From the August Fields collection

X-large bag

Exterior A:
HDABS-13 Coreopsis
Color: Green
From the August Fields collection

Exterior B:
HDABS-13 Coreopsis
Color: Spruce
From the August Fields collection

Lining:
HDABS-09 Knot Garden
Color: Celery
From the August Fields collection

BEAUTIFUL BALANCE CHECKBOOK COVER (PAGE 55)

Exterior flap:
HDABS-18
Color: Mint
From the Home Dec Solids collection

Exterior:
HDABS-14 Bright Buds
Color: Brick
From the August Fields collection

Lining:
HDABS-10 Sunrise
Color: Seafoam
From the August Fields collection

PERFECTLY PLEATED CLUTCH (PAGE 65)

Small bag

Exterior pleated panel:
AB-42 Dandelion Field
Color: Forest
From the Daisy Chain collection

Exterior bands/handle:
AB-31 Ripple Stripe
Color: Green
From the Midwest Modern 2 collection

Lining:
AB-29 Happy Dots
Color: Yellow
From the Midwest Modern 2 collection

Medium bag

Exterior pleated panel:
AB-26 Martini
Color: Mustard
From the Midwest Modern collection

Exterior bands/handle:
AB-23 Garden Maze
Color: Grey
From the Midwest Modern collection

Lining:
AB-29 Happy Dots
Color: Grey
From the Midwest Modern collection

Large bag (as seen on page 77)

Exterior pleated panel:
AB-39 Pressed Flowers
Color: Turquoise
From the Daisy Chain collection

Exterior bands/handle:
AB-38 Daisy Bouquet
Color: Indigo
From the Daisy Chain collection

Lining:
AB-35 Mosaic
Color: River
From the Daisy Chain collection

TEARDROP BAG (PAGE 79)

Small bag

Exterior main panel:
AB-28 Trailing Cherries
Color: Brown
From the Midwest Modern collection

Exterior bands/strap:
AB-29 Happy Dots
Color: Apricot
From the Midwest Modern collection

Lining:
AB-45
Color: Hot Pink
From the quilting-weight Solids collection

Large bag

Exterior main panel:
AB-39 Pressed Flowers
Color: Forest
From the Daisy Chain collection

Exterior bands/strap:
AB-42 Dandelion Field
Color: Grey
From the Daisy Chain collection

Lining:
AB-37 Kaleidoscope Dots
Color: Natural
From the Daisy Chain collection

Large bag (as seen on page 89)

Main panel:
AB-39 Pressed Flowers
Color: Forest
From the Daisy Chain collection

Straps/hips:
AB-42 Dandelion Field
Color: Grey
From the Daisy Chain collection

KEY KEEPER COIN PURSE (PAGE 91)

Exterior main panel:
AB-28 Trailing Cherries
Color: Brown
From the Midwest Modern collection

Exterior bands/strap:
AB-29 Garden Maze
Color: Mustard
From the Midwest Modern collection

Lining:
AB-45
Color: Fuchsia
From the quilting-weight Solids collection

FRINGED HOBO BAG (PAGE 101)

Small shoulder bag

Exterior main/handle:
AB-29 Happy Dots
Color: Grey
From the Midwest Modern 2 collection

Yoke:
AB-39 Pressed Flowers
Color: Rose
From the Daisy Chain collection

Lining:
AB-23 Garden Maze
Color: Sand
From the Midwest Modern 2 collection

Large handbag (as seen on page 111)

Exterior main/handle:
HDABS-12 Full Bloom
Color: Moss
From the August Fields collection

Yoke:
HDABS-15 Frest Start
Color: Moss
From the August Fields collection

Lining:
HDABS-11 Graceful Vine
Color: Spruce
From the August Fields collection

BLOSSOM HANDBAG/SHOULDER BAG (PAGE 113)

Handbag

Exterior:
HDABS-14 Bright Buds
Color: Grey
From the August Fields collection

Lining:
HDABS-09 Knot Garden
Color: Celery
From the August Fields collection

Dividers:
AB-45
Color: Grey
From the quilting-weight Solids collection

Shoulder bag

Exterior:
HDABS-17 Dream Poppies
Color: Tangerine
From the August Fields collection

Lining:
HDABS-14 Bright Buds
Color: Chocolate
From the August Fields collection

Dividers:
AB-45
Color: Ivory
From the quilting-weight Solids collection

Shoulder bag (as seen on page 8, top right)

Exterior
HDABS-24 Trumpet Flowers
Color: Emerald
From the Love collection

EVERYTHING WRISTLET (PAGE 127)

Small wristlet

Exterior flap:
AB-30 Nouveau Trees
Color: Moss
From the Midwest Modern collection

Exterior main panel:
AB-45
Color: Lime
From the quilting-weight Solids collection

Lining:
AB-30 Happy Dots
Color: Pink
From the Midwest Modern collection

Large wristlet

Exterior flap:
AB-45
Color: Slate
From the quilting-weight Solids collection

Exterior main panel:
AB31 Ripple Stripe
Color: Grey
From the Midwest Modern 2 collection

Lining:
AB-45
Color: Fuchsia
From the quilting-weight Solids collection

MISS MAVEN RUFFLED HANDBAG (PAGE 141)

Medium handbag

Exterior main panel:
AB-32 Fresh Poppies
Color: Green
From the Midwest Modern collection

Exterior handles/ruffle:
AB-45
Color: Green
From the quilting-weight Solids collection

Lining:
AB-23 Garden Maze
Color: Green
From the Midwest Modern collection

Large handbag

Exterior main panel:
AB-40 Sweet Jasmine
Color: Navy
From the Daisy Chain collection

Exterior handles/ruffle:
AB-38 Daisy Bouquet
Color: Turquoise
From the Daisy Chain collection

Lining:
AB-38 Daisy Bouquet
Color: Indigo
From the Daisy Chain collection

Exterior main panel (as seen on page 155):
AB-50 Bliss Bouquet
Color: Teal
From the Love collection

Handles/ruffle
AB-46 Sunspots
Color: Tangerine
From the Love collection

TAKE FLIGHT HANDBAG/SHOULDER BAG (PAGE 157)

Handbag (as seen on page 169)

Exterior side/bottom/handles:
HDABS-18
Color: Sage
From the Home Dec Solids collection

Exterior front/back main panels/lining:
HDABS-18
Color: Leaf
From the Home Dec Solids collection

Petals:
AB-33 Floating Buds
Color: Sage

AB-23 Garden Maze
Color: Olive
From the Midwest Modern collection

Trim:
AB-45
Color: Ivory
From the quilting-weight Solids collection

Shoulder bag

Exterior side/bottom/handles:
HDABS-18
Color: Grey
From the Home Dec Solids collection

Exterior front/back main panels/lining:
HDABS-18
Color: Ivory
From the Home Dec Solids collection

Petals:
AB-40 Sweet Jasmine
Color: Grey

AB-38 Daisy Bouquet
Color: Mist
From the Daisy Chain collection

Trim:
AB-45
Color: Mist
From the quilting-weight Solids collection

Acknowledgments

It is a total pleasure and joy to dedicate this book to the passionate souls who love sewing and crafting. Your enthusiasm and creativity inspire all!

Special thanks to some amazing folks for your contributions—this book is possible because of you. Thank you for your collaboration and constant support: David Butler for your love, care, sense of humor, and sage advice. Dianne Barcus for your nonstop talent and dedication; you are my compass. Jake Redinger and Kim Ventura for your instructions and illustration genius! This book is all the richer because of you. Diane Capaci, "Miss Wonderful," for organizing our lives and the studio. Joy Jung, Anna Aschenbeck, Suzanne Aschenbeck, Kerri Thomson, and Nichole Redinger for your gorgeous testing and sewing abilities. Miss Nora Corbet for her fantastic styling support. All of the models for sharing their beautiful energy: Drenda Cline, Heather Corwin, Christina Medrick, Jesse Smith, Rebecca Smith, Holly Struthers, Taylor Struthers, and Marie Shuttleworth. Sarah Bailey, Joyce Robertson, and the whole team at Westminster Fibers for your friendship and nonstop supply of fabrics! Nancy Jewell at Coats and Clark for copious amounts of thread and zips. Rolando Berdion, Michele Stanganelli, and Pellon for yards of interfacing. Patricia Zelek of Prym-Dritz for great bag closures. Caroline and Marc for your warmth, inspiration, and guidance. Dolin O'Shea for your technical clarity. Aya Akazawa for art direction extraordinaire. Kate Woodrow, Carleigh Bell, and Laura Lee Mattingly for keeping things in the flow. Christina Loff and Nancy Deane for your marketing and promotion expertise. And Jodi Warshaw for your thoughtful vision and presence. Thank you all so much.

xo Amy

Resources

I hope you're having a good time with my projects! Like you, I'm always on the lookout for great materials. Here's a list of resources to help you discover new ideas and inspiration. Enjoy!

SOURCES FOR FABRICS AND NOTIONS

For a selection of the finest niche fabric retailers, please visit www.amybutlerdesign.com; search under Where to Buy for a retailer near you. Through these purveyors, you will find thousands of beautiful fabrics, as well as my fabric designs from Rowan. You will also find incredible educational opportunities and great personal service.

Visit www.westminsterfibers.com to see their full offering of amazing fabrics from their designers; you can also search on the site for retailers near you.

RETAIL STORES

Anthropologie
www.anthropologie.com
A great source of fashion items and textiles perfect for repurposing.

Bell'occhio
www.bellocchio.com
Collections of antique trims, fabrics, and ephemera.

eBay
www.ebay.com
Several online auctions and store sites for fabrics, notions, and trims.

Etsy
www.etsy.com
Home to thousands of craft and design resources and shops. Great selection of new and vintage materials.

Fabric Farms
www.fabricfarms.com
Great home dec fabrics, amazing trims.

Fairfield
www.poly-fil.com
My source for premium fillers and batting. Click on Where to Buy to find a retailer near you.

French General
www.frenchgeneral.com
Special notions, trims, and textiles.

Green Velvet
www.mygreenvelvet.com
An incredible selection of fabrics, beads, buttons, trims, vintage milliner flora, and ribbons—both vintage and new!

GREAT CRAFT WEB SITES AND BLOGS FOR INFORMATION AND INSPIRATION

Hancock Fabrics
www.hancockfabrics.com
A great source of notions and sewing supplies.

Harmony Art
www.harmonyart.com
Beautiful organic fabrics.

Hobby Lobby
www.hobbylobby.com
Notions, sewing supplies, and tools.

Jo-Ann Stores, Inc.
www.joann.com.
A good selection of notions and sewing supplies.

Nancy's Notions
www.nancysnotions.com
A great source of notions and specialty fabrics.

Pellon
www.pellonideas.com
The go-to source for several interfacings and
materials used in this book.

Salsa Fabrics
www.salsafabrics.com
Unusual imported fabrics.

Sobo Style
www.sobostyle.com
A unique selection of fabrics and gifts, old
and new.

Urban Outfitters
www.urbanoutfitters.com
A good source of modern print bedspreads and
curtains, great for repurposing.

www.africankelli.com

www.apartmenttherapy.com

www.annamariahorner.blogspot.com

www.craftster.org

www.craftyplanet.com

www.craftzine.com

www.decor8.blogspot.com

www.dioramarama.com

www.getcrafty.com

www.greenkitchen.com

www.patternreview.com

www.purlbee.com

www.quiltersbuzz.com

www.readymade.com

www.selvedge.org

www.sfgirlbybay.blogspot.com

www.stacysews.com

www.stylebakery.com

www.tinagivens.blogspot.com

www.u-handbag.com

www.whipup.net

www.worstedwitch.com

Index

te
ba
Th
Re
Fi
in
h

Le

r